Published by Ferry Publications © 2005
PO Box 33, Ramsey, Isle of Man, IM99 LP Tel: +44 (0) 1624 898445   Fax: +44 (0) 1624 898449
E-mail: FerryPubs@aol.com   Website: www.ferrypubs.co.uk

The former *Horsa*, seen as the *Express Penelope*, approaching the Greek port of Rafina in February 2003, prior to her disposal by Hellas Ferries. (Richard Seville)

Introduction

O ne of the fascinating aspects of an interest in ferries is the numerous different ways people approach the topic. Some like only to photograph the ships, others find the technical side interesting, some people concentrate exclusively on a particular company, port or route – I could go on and on. Personally, the aspect I enjoy the most is tracking down vessels that have been sold on from UK waters – seeing how they have changed, both externally and internally, and searching for vestiges of their previous guises.

My interest began with annual holidays in the mid-to-late 1980s with DFDS and later Scandinavian Seaways. To a 7-year old, an overnight crossing on the *Tor Britannia* was hugely exciting and made a significant impression upon me. How I looked forward to those voyages – I recall writing a fan letter to DFDS requesting a bridge visit, which was kindly permitted. My growing interest was confirmed with a return crossing on the *Stena Horsa* on Christmas Eve 1991, just prior to the closure of the Folkestone to Boulogne route and the Folkestone sisters have remained my favourite vessels ever since.

Throughout the 1990s I wondered what had happened to the *Hengist* and *Horsa*, and thrived on any news snippets that came along. When the opportunity of a Greek holiday came along in June 1999, I was determined to track them down, and during that first visit managed to sail on the *Panagia Ekatontapiliani*. The former *Hengist* was at that time barely changed inside. Thus began my fascination in searching out former UK-based vessels, which has led to travel throughout Europe, particularly in the Mediterranean.

Sylvester the Cat! The *Moby Drea's* striking funnel colours, September 2004. *(Richard Seville)*

Rivals the **Penelope A** and the **Superferry II**, both former Ostend ships, seen at Mykonos' old harbour, in July 2005. *(Richard Seville)*

The pursuit has been great fun and has opened up places and cultures that I would never have otherwise experienced. From the cosmopolitan Ibiza Town to the foreboding port of Vlore, from the chaotic souk in Tangier to the alluring tranquillity of the Croatian islands. There have however, certainly been moments when I have doubted my sanity – waiting for a connection at 04.00 on a dark, freezing cold February morning at Tinos, or walking ashore amidst baying Alsatians, rusting cranes and aggressive touts in Albania.

As well as sampling the vessels, I also enjoy photographing them.

This book aims to bring together some of my best photographs, to publish them alongside comparative views from their UK days so that everyone can see how the ships have changed.

I hope you enjoy them.

Richard Seville
Kingston-upon-Thames
August 2005.

PREFACE

Former UK ferries can be found in active service throughout the world – in the Americas and the Caribbean, Australasia, the Far and Middle East. However, whilst many have also found renewed employment in Scandinavia, by far the greatest concentration of ex-UK tonnage is in the Mediterranean. Indeed, the tonnage cascade has long seen UK ferries migrate south to find further employment – where in the past, the operators, traffic and infrastructure was less developed. Although events in the 1990s have definitely challenged this tradition - with an influx of superb, purpose-built tonnage – in 2005 the Mediterranean is still home to a large collection of second-hand vessels.

NEW HOMES

Until the 1960s, when UK operators had finished with their older tonnage, it was common practise that these ferries would be sold for breaking. Some were sold on for further service, but these were a minority. As the 1960s and 1970s unrolled, however, more and more redundant passenger ferries began to be sold for active employment – principally to the Mediterranean – and particularly to Greece. Swedish Lloyd's *Suecia* and *Britannia* of 1929 went to Hellenic Mediterranean in 1966, both British Rail's *Amsterdam* and the IOMSP's *Mona's Queen* went to Chandris for cruising whilst SNCF's crack *Lisieux* and Sealink's *St Patrick* and *Hibernia* were all sold to Agapitos Bros during the 1970s. However, it was not until the first generation of purpose-built car ferries were replaced, that the flow of second-hand tonnage to the Mediterranean really increased. The market was initially concentrated in the Eastern Mediterranean, where Greece – with her extensive network of islands – was the major buyer. Numerous early car ferries were sold here – the *Sappho*, *Tor Hollandia*, *Free Enterprise 1*, *St George*…. the list of familiar names goes on and on. Enterprising Greek ship-owners could transform these tired ships and revitalise them for many more years of service.

As new private operators were established to challenge dominant nationalised concerns, further markets were created for former UK tonnage – notably in Italy, where both Moby Lines and Tourship's Corsica Ferries both purchased extensive second-hand fleets, and where archipelagos such as those in the Bay of Naples provide valuable employment for smaller ships too. Whilst there was once a distinct lack of former UK tonnage in the Western Mediterranean, the 1990s saw ready purchasers emerge in both Spain and Morocco, where traffic is fuelled by vast numbers of emigrant north African families annually returning home. The Balkan crisis provoked expansion of the long trades from Italy to Turkey as traffic avoided the region where migrant families returning home also needed cheap passage, thus creating a seasonal need for older tonnage. Now peace has returned, demand for second-hand ferries is booming to serve countries such as Croatia, Montenegro and Albania. Today, therefore, ex-UK tonnage can be found right across the Mediterranean. From sheltered water crossings to island hops or long, overnight hauls - old friends can be found in a wide variety of fascinating trades. Key clusters of tonnage are currently found in the Spain to

Morocco trade across the Straits of Gibraltar, on the southern Adriatic, in the Greek Cyclades and Dodecanese archipelagos and along Italy's west coast. Some of the ferries are barely altered, others are hardly recognisable – the majority are changed gradually over successive refits, but inevitably there will always be some trace of their past if you look hard enough.

CONTINUED DEMAND

It is questionable, however, how long second-hand UK tonnage will continue to be so prolific in the Mediterranean. Until GA Ferries' purchase of the *PO Kent* in 2003, it had been six years since a UK passenger ferry had been sold to Greek owners. Numerous Mediterranean operators that may once have been interested in the second-hand market are now building outstanding ferries of their own – Minoan Lines, Blue Star Ferries (the former Strinzis Lines), Moby Lines and Corsica Ferries for instance. As companies convert to high-speed operations, they purchase new craft as opposed to older tonnage – Lineas Fred. Olsen, Medmar (previously Linee Lauro) and the former Hellas Flying Dolphin group are all prime examples.

Legal restrictions have also impacted one of the biggest markets. Whilst logic dictates that it is maintenance standards that determine the life of a ship, obsession with safety is also piling on pressure – particularly in Greece. Reference is made in this book to the 35-year rule whereby any vessel on the Greek register engaged in domestic trades must be retired after the season in which it reaches its 35th year. At the end of 2004, this rule forced the premature retirement of the former *Vortigern*,

which otherwise could have provided several more years' valuable service. The Greek Government seems to equate age directly with the safety of a ship – which is not at all the case, as numerous Greek ship-owners have previously demonstrated. It does, however, become a self-fulfilling prophecy with operators cutting costs on vessels they know there is no point in maintaining. The situation currently looks set to worsen, with the 35-year limit now decreasing each year on a rolling basis until a new 30-year limit is reached in 2008.

Greek ship-owners are strongly opposed to this move, which will have a dramatic effect on their fleets. Some compromise is likely, but nothing is guaranteed. If the rule is implemented, favourites such as the *Horsa* and *St Columba* will be forcibly retired by 2006 and 2008 respectively. A maximum 20-year rule was also mooted for entry into onto the Greek register, but this has quietly been dropped. The 35-year rule applies only to domestic Greek ferries – and not to Greek-owned ships engaged in international trades. Hence it is not applicable in the trans-Adriatic routes, but aside from the southern-most routes from Brindisi or Bari, it is this market that has seen a heavy influx of purpose-built ships.

REDUCED SUPPLY?

Not only has the Mediterranean market for second-hand tonnage contracted, but the supply is also much reduced too. The capacity and facilities evolution has stabilised whilst the economic reality of the Channel Tunnel, the end of duty-free sales and the advent of budget airlines have all hit ferry companies hard. Trends now show

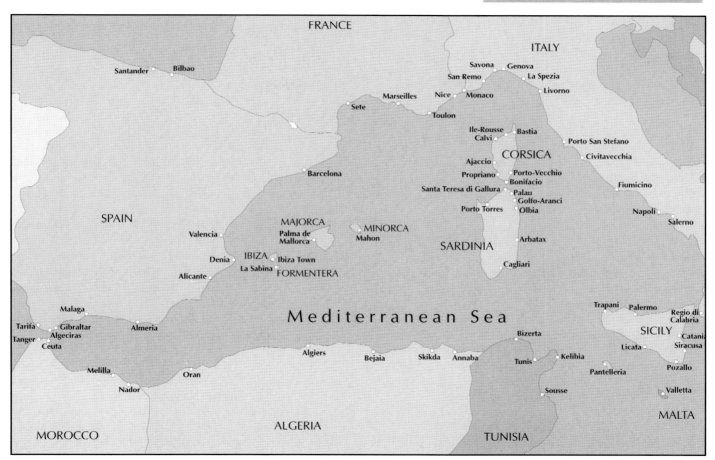

UK operators retaining their tonnage far longer than they may have done previously – DFDS being a prime example. Even if Mediterranean operators want the tonnage, it may not be readily available in future. By the time ships are available, they are too old to be attractive to Mediterranean operators – the recent sales of P&O Scottish Ferries' *St Clair* and *St Sunniva* and P&O Portsmouth's *Pride of Hampshire* and *Pride of Cherbourg* direct to Middle-Eastern buyers are example cases. This market has previously been at the very end of the tonnage cascade but now ferries are being sold directly to the region as there is no demand in the Mediterranean.

Today, there are few European areas where veteran ships are really in demand – the Albanian crossings are perhaps the last remaining market where 'rust buckets' can eek out their final days.

At the other end of the scale, it had also often been thought that more recent UK tonnage was simply becoming too large to be useful in the Mediterranean – particularly in the islands – but recent sales have proved this is not the case. Although infrastructure does not exist to support double vehicle deck loading, this has not prevented the purchase of ships such as the *PO Kent* – GA Ferries have simply installed a large ramp to enable access to the upper level.

The Mediterranean is currently a rich hunting ground for those interested in former UK ferries – and it is more easily accessible than ever. Those budget airlines damaging the ferry industry in the UK also permit relatively cheap visits to southern Europe – where, with the exception of Spain, typical ferry fares are decidedly cheaper than in the UK. It is without doubt a great time to seek out old friends and it is highly recommended – before the variety of the scene disappears.

ACKNOWLEDGMENTS

I owe thanks to many people who have kindly helped with the preparation of this book. Firstly, my travelling companion Matt Murtland, who provided the initial idea for this book and kindly proofread the text, and whose company has been greatly valued during our trips to track down these ferries. I must express my gratitude to Bruce Peter and Geoff Hamer for their regular information and clarification, and to John Hendy and Miles Cowsill for supporting this project. Thanks are also due to the following – Micke Asklander, whose website www.faktaomfartyg.com is highly recommended, Gary Andrews, Clive Harvey, John May, Bill Mayes, Andreas Worteler, Marko Stampehl and Nikos Thryos.

Captured in the new Hellenic Seaways livery, the **Express Santorini** is seen at Piraeus during July 2005. *(Richard Seville)*

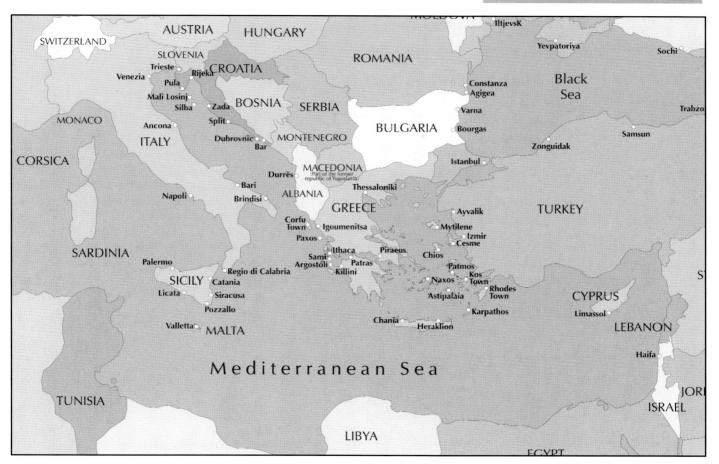

ANTRIM PRINCESS 1967 – 1986
Tynwald 1986 – 1990
1967 – Hawthorn Leslie, Newcastle-upon-Tyne, UK

The *Antrim Princess* was the British Railway Board's first-ever drive-through car ferry. Initially ordered for the Caledonian Steam Packet Company (Irish) Services Ltd., controversially she was delivered in 1967 in full BRB livery. She was to serve the Stranraer to Larne route until late 1985, when chartered to become the new flagship of the Isle of Man Steam Packet. She ran from Heysham to Douglas as the *Tynwald* until 1990 when her fate was sealed by new government regulations concerning stability, which she did not meet. Returned to Sealink British Ferries she was laid up on the River Fal until sold to Naples-based

The *Lauro Express* seen in Naples in July 2003, dwarfed by the cruise ship *Legend of the Seas* alongside. *(Richard Seville)*

The former *Antrim Princess* is seen here as the *Tynwald* arriving at Heysham during her career with the Isle of Man Steam Packet Company. *(Miles Cowsill)*

Linee Lauro. The Italian operator rebuilt her as an overnight vessel, adding cabins in the entire aft half of her main passenger deck. As the *Lauro Express* she was used on a variety of services linking Italy, Corsica, Sardinia and even Tunisia – the latter involving voyages of up to 29 hours! Following frictions within the controlling families during 2002, the Lauro-group operations were split up, and she joined the Medmar fleet under the D'Abundo family. To re-inforce this move she was renamed the *Giuseppe D'Abundo* in early 2004, but with the closure of Medmar's Sete to Palma route she was indirectly replaced and spent much of 2004 laid up in Naples. A proposed new service for 2005 from Bari to Dubrovnik failed to materialise and she was instead chartered out to D&P Ferries for service in Albania.

ARGO Various from 1976 –1991
Norcove 1991 – 1994
Sally Euroway 1995 - 1997
1976 – Krogerwerft GmBH, Rendsburg, Germany.

Until passing to Iscomar Ferries for their Barcelona to Palma route, the *Argo* had spent virtually her entire career on different short-term charters. This nomadic existence however led her to become extremely well known around the UK, as she served no less than four different operators – North Sea Ferries, Olau Line, P&O European Ferries and lastly Sally Line. She was renamed the *Norcove* during a three-year charter to North Sea Ferries from

The *Iscomarís Patricia del Mar* heads out of Palma de Majorca in August 2003. *(Richard Seville)*

The freight vessel **Sally Euroway** inward bound from Ostend to Ramsgate. *(FotoFlite)*

1991 to 1994, and became the *Sally Euroway* between 1995 and 1997 after which she sailed from Ramsgate to Ostend as Sally Direct's *Euroway*. Although founded in 1979, Iscomar did not enter passenger traffic until 1998 but have steadily expanded in this sector since. The *Patricia del Mar* inaugurated the Barcelona connection upon acquisition in 2002 offering a ro-pax service. She remained on the link until 2004, when released by the new *Mercedes del Mar* and used to commence a new route from Valencia to Palma. The Iscomar fleet was swelled with another vessel from former UK waters in 2005, with the arrival of the Emeraude Line's ferry the *Solidor 4* as the *Pitivsa Nova*.

BREIZH-IZEL 1980 – 1989
1970 – Taikoo Dockyard, Hong Kong

Best known in UK waters as Brittany Ferries freighter *Breizh-Izel*, the *Duchess M* was actually constructed for service in New Zealand for the Union Steamship Co. The company foundered in 1976 and she was subsequently sold to Greek interests to operate as the *Iniochos Express* before being acquired by Brittany Ferries in 1980. Deployed both from Plymouth and Portsmouth, she was transferred to British Channel Island Ferries in 1986, a company in which Brittany Ferries owned a substantial stake. She again headed to the Mediterranean in 1989 when sold to the expanding Marlines, effectively replacing the former fleet mate *Penn-ar-Bed* from the fleet. Renamed the *Duchess M*, she was substantially extended aft to make her suitable for full passenger operations, including an upper vehicle deck served by lift. Marlines suffered heavily against the new tonnage that debuted on the Adriatic in the mid to late 1990s, and in 1999 it appeared they had ceased operations when their remaining fleet, including the *Duchess M*, was seemingly sold to Lebanese interests. The *Duchess M* was renamed the *Balbek*, but re-appeared in 2000 for Marlines on a service from Bari to Igoumenitsa. 2001 saw the company withdraw from the Greece to Italy trade in order to operate to Montenegro, initially to Kotor and subsequently to Bar. The *Duchess M* regained her former name the same year and although services are highly sporadic, she has since re-appeared each summer as the last reminder of Marlines' once extensive operation. (see page 18 for comparative photo)

British Channel Island Ferries' **Brizh-Izel** approaches Portsmouth harbour inward bound from Jersey. *(Miles Cowsill)*

CARISBROOKE CASTLE 1959 – 1974
1959 - J. Thornycroft & Co., Southampton, UK

The *Carisbrooke Castle* arrived in 1959 as Red Funnel's first ever purpose-built car ferry. Sailing between Southampton and both East and West Cowes, she was joined by a near-sister in 1962 and two further similar vessels followed. In 1974 she was displaced by the new *Netley Castle* and sold to Italian interests to become the *Citta di Meta*. Put into operation between Naples and Ischia, she spent fifteen years in this trade until sold in 1989 to Maregiglio for service to the small Tyrrhenian island of Giglio. Renamed the *Giglio Espresso Secondo*, she sailed on the hour-long crossing to the mainland port of Porto S. Stefano until 2000. At 41 years of age, further employment may have appeared unlikely, but she was sold again for active service, passing to the Sardinian firm

The *Giglio Espresso II* en-route to La Maddelena in September 2004. *(Richard Seville)*

The *Carisbrooke Castle* was the first purpose-built Red Funnel car ferry and is seen leaving Cowes for Southampton in 1965. *(John Hendy)*

Tremar without a change of name. Initially used between Carloforte and Calasetta, she was later transferred to the competitive 15-minute run from Palau to La Maddelena island. In profile, she is remarkably little altered from new, with just slight extensions to her accommodation. Her facilities are today extremely basic, with an open-plan saloon and bar forward almost entirely devoid of seating and further sparse lounge space aft – although this is adequate for the short crossing. Despite intense competition, Tremar appear well patronised, but in late 2004 the company was taken over by larger rival Enermar. What this means for the *Giglio Espresso II* is unclear – but is would seem unlikely there is a long term place for her in the merged fleets as Enermar already operate much more modern tonnage.

CHARTRES 1974 - 1993
1974 - Dubignon-Normandie SA, Nantes, France

Delivered in 1974 to SNCF, the French partners in the Sealink consortium, the *Chartres* was the second derivation of the multi-purpose design first seen in British Rail's *Vortigern* (q.v). During a 19-year career on the English Channel she saw varied service - initially based on the short-sea crossings from Dover to both Calais and Dunkirk, she spent the majority of the 1980s on the Newhaven to Dieppe route. Following replacement by the *Champs Elysees* in 1990, she returned to Dover to operate the rail-connected summer sailings to Calais, a role she fulfilled until 1993. At the end of the 1993 season, she was sold to Agapitos Express Ferries of Greece to replace the former Belgian stalwart, the *Artevelde*, on the central Cycladic trunk from Piraeus to Paros, Naxos, Ios and Santorini. Renamed the *Express Santorini*, her sun decks were extended aft to cater for the large number of deck passengers on this popular route. Although she initially entered Greek service with her interior essentially unaltered, in the late 1990s she was comprehensively refurbished and now boasts extremely comfortable facilities with

SNCF's versatile passenger/car/train ferry **Chartres** speeding away from Calais in 1981. *(John Hendy)*

Captured in late afternoon sunshine, the **Express Santorini** is seen in the Saronic Gulf in October 2002 enroute to the Cyclades. *(Richard Seville)*

laminate flooring and contemporary fittings throughout. New en-suite cabins were also installed in former crew areas on her bridge deck. Vestiges of her past do remain, however, with a large painting of Dieppe harbour in her forward stairwell and a wooden bas-relief of Chartres cathedral in her upper forward lounge. In late 1999, Agapitos Express Ferries were one of the several firms merged into the new Hellas Ferries operation, which initially dominated domestic traffic. In recent years their operations have been severely cut back, but despite the early retirement of fleet mates, the *Express Santorini* remains a mainstay of their operations. In 2005 she continues on the central Cycladic route under the new Hellenic Seaways brand name.

CITY OF YORK 1953 - 1971
1953 – Vickers Armstrong, Newcastle, UK

Admittedly not strictly a UK ferry, but certainly a British passenger vessel that did become a most significant Greek ferry. The *City of York* was built in 1953 for Ellerman's routes from London to Beira, via the West Coast of Africa. By 1971 she had become out-dated due to containerisation, and could easily have followed many combi-passenger-cargo liners of the time to the breakers, but instead she was sold to Karageorgis Lines of Greece. At Perama she was radically transformed into a car-ferry with a striking modern appearance, although many of her original

The magnificent looking **City of York** heads down the English Channel during her career with Ellerman's. *(FotoFlite)*

wooden fixtures were retained and re-used in the rebuild. It was not until 1974 that she made her debut on Karageorgis' Ancona to Rhodes service as the *Mediterranean Sky*, sailing in tandem with her sister, the *City of Exeter* that had also been rebuilt as the *Mediterranean Sea*. At the time of her debut, the Karageorgis ferries were far superior to their rivals, and the company was a leading Adriatic operator throughout the 1970s and early 1980s. However, a lack of investment meant they fell behind and by the mid-1990s the company was in serious trouble, with their ageing vessels particularly hampered by slow speeds and low freight capacity compared to their aggressive rivals. In 1994 the vessel was chartered to the US military and deployed to both the Somalia and Haiti crises. Upon her return she was linked with a number of ventures that failed to materialise, before the collapse of Karageorgis in August 1997 saw her occupied by her crew at Patras. She remained there until February 1999 when towed to Elefsis and laid up. It was there in November 2002 that she broke loose from her moorings and capsized in shallow water just to the west of Petrola. The wreck remains in situ today, until recently under the watchful eye of the nearby *Margarita L*, formerly the *Windsor Castle*.

The **Mediterranean Sky** lies on her side in a bay close to Petrola, Elefsis Bay, in February 2003. *(Richard Seville)*

The *Duchess M* is seen approaching the Montenegrin port of Bar during July 2003. *(Richard Seville)*

Jadrolinija's *Dubrovnik* prepares to berth at Stari Grad, Hvar island, July 2003. *(Richard Seville)*

CONNACHT 1978 – 1988
Duchesse Anne 1988 – 1996
1978 – Verolme Dockyard, Cork, Ireland

The *Connacht* was delivered to Ireland's B+I Line for their Cork to Swansea service. In 1980, she was switched to the overnight route from Dublin to Liverpool, operating an additional daytime round trip to Holyhead instead of lying over in Dublin. With the nationalised operator under increasing financial pressure, the *Connacht* was sold in 1988 to Brittany Ferries, for whom she debuted in 1989 as the *Duchesse Anne*. Predominantly associated with services to St Malo, she was offered for sale in 1996 at a time when Brittany Ferries themselves were in financial difficulty. She

was sold to Croatian-national operator Jadrolinija, whose services were once-again beginning to expand following the tragic war that had engulfed the Balkan state. As the Dubrovnik, she joined the *Marko Polo* (q.v.) to become the mainstay of Jadrolinija's international and fast-coastal services, alternating between the two. The latter run the length of the Croatian coastline, from Rijeka in the North to Dubrovnik in the South, calling en route at various island and mainland ports, and offering the most spectacular scenic crossings in southern Europe – at value fares. On board, she is utterly unchanged from Brittany Ferries days, but is maintained in immaculate condition throughout.

B&I Line's distinctive looking *Connacht* is seen here inward bound from Rosslare to Pembroke Dock off Angle Bay, Pembrokeshire. *(Miles Cowsill)*

The *Dubrovnik* is seen holding off the island of Korcula, June 2004. *(Richard Seville)*

Transado's battered **Mira Praia** approaches Troia in July 2002. *(Richard Seville)*

Moby Lines' *Moby Love* shows her new bow visor whilst berthed at Portaferraio in September 2004. The former *Coruisk* is seen to the left as the *Lampomare Uno*. (Richard Seville)

CORUISK 1969 - 1986
1969 – Ailsa Shipyard, Troon, UK

The diminutive *Coruisk* is perhaps the least likely vessel to feature in this book. Constructed in 1969 for the Caledonian Steam Packet's Isle of Skye services, she was replaced in 1971 by the new *Kyleakin* and *Lochalsh*. She was then converted to bow loading prior to inaugurating the Largs to Cumbrae Slip route, gaining Caledonian MacBrayne colours in 1973 upon the CSP's merger with David MacBrayne. Although the new Isl*e of Cumbrae* arrived in 1977, she remained principally stationed at Largs until 1986 when displaced from the fleet by the first of the new Loch-class. The following two years are somewhat of a mystery, but in

The *Lampomare Uno* at her lay-by berth in Portaferraio, September 2004. *(Richard Seville)*

1988 she appeared at the Italian island of Elba having been acquired by Lampogas. A leading Italian LPG producer, Lampogas purchased her to transport their hazardous LGP tankers to and from the island. Renamed the *Lampomare Uno* and repainted entirely in their trademark bright yellow colour scheme, she greatly adds to an already diverse local fleet, which also includes Sealink's former *Earl Godwin* (q.v) and *Saint Eloi* (q.v.), as well as Sally Line's *The Viking*. The *Lampomare Uno* does not operate a set schedule, but sails as and when required. During the day, she can usually be found lying over in a corner of Portaferraio harbour.

The *Coruisk* leaves the seaside town of Largs. *(Ian Hall)*

CUTHRED 1969 - 1987
1969 – Richards, Lowestoft, UK

Built for the Portsmouth to Fishbourne route, the *Cuthred* was to remain on this crossing for her entire Sealink career. Her delivery in 1969 presented a substantially different profile on the route, as for the first time, the passenger accommodation spanned the car deck. Three half-sisters were delivered in 1973, with the *Caedmon* serving alongside the *Cuthred* at Portsmouth. Notoriously underpowered, the *Cuthred* was relegated to reserve vessel in 1983 when the first two Saint-class arrived. In 1988 she was sold to Newcastle-based operators who intended to remodel her to sail as a Mississippi-style river cruiser. Perhaps

The *Mira Praia* seen alongside at Troia in July 2002. *(Richard Seville)*

The unsuccessful **Cuthred** was the first railway-owned Isle of Wight car ferry with accommodation built over her vehicle deck. *(John Hendy collection)*

unsurprisingly, these plans did not come to fruition and, unaltered, she was resold in 1989 to Transado for use on their 15-minute link between Sebutal and Troia, south of Lisbon. As the *Mira Praia*, the former *Cuthred* was re-united with her one-time Sealink fleet mate *Camber Queen*, which served as the *Mira Troia* until broken up in 2000. The *Mira Praia* remains in regular service, although conditions on board are rather depressing. The cafe-bar has been entirely stripped out, and facilities now consist simply of row-upon-row of hard seating. The seating, bulkheads and even ceiling were covered in graffiti during the author's last trip, with Sealink's ubiquitous black patterned formica not enhancing the atmosphere!

The **Derin Deniz** captured at Brindisi during her short-lived service to Turkey, July 2003. *(Richard Seville)*

A sunlit *Kapetan Alexandros A* enters Brindisiis inner harbour during July 2004. *(Richard Seville)*

DANA FUTURA 1975 – 1975
Dana Futura 1977 - 1988
1975 - Helsingors Vaerft, Helsingor, Denmark

The *Polaris* was built as the *Dana Futura* for DFDS' North Sea freight route from Esbjerg to Harwich. However, within four months of delivery she had been chartered out and her early career with DFDS was to be characterised by numerous periods chartered to other operators and only sporadic service on the route she was ordered for. Having been lengthened in 1985, she was sold in 1988 to Nordo Link for use between Helsingborg and Travemunde. Additional cabin accommodation was added and she was renamed the *Skane Link*. She remained on this service until late 1991 when sold to Ventouris Ferries, one of several operations under the Ventouris name each run by a different Ventouris brother. Ventouris Ferries' services were concentrated on the southern Adriatic, linking

Ventouris Ferriesí *Polaris* departs Bari against leaden skies, April 2002. *(Richard Seville)*

Patras, Igoumenitsa and Bari. Although freight-orientated, passengers are carried and her accommodation was extended further before entering service as the *Polaris*. Her acquisition by Ventouris Ferries meant reunion with her sister, the *Dana Gloria*, which had been purchased in 1990 and was then sailing as the *Venus*. Although other Ventouris companies have since collapsed, Ventouris Ferries continues to survive despite intense modern competition. However, financial difficulties did see the *Polaris* chartered back to Nordo Link between 1998 and 2000. She subsequently served Cotunav before returning to year-round operation for her owners in 2001. With the contraction of the Ventouris Ferries once-large fleet, the *Polaris* - together with her sister, now renamed the *Siren* – are the mainstays of the route, which no longer continues to Patras. The route's emphasis remains on heavy-freight traffic and passenger facilities are decidedly basic.

The DFDS vessel **Dana Futura** was built for the freight service linking Esbjerg and Harwich but quickly found plenty of charter work. *(John Hendy collection)*

The **Doric Ferry** is seen here off the Isle of Arran undergoing trials prior to entering service for the Atlantic Steam Navigation Company. *(Miles Cowsill collection)*

DORIC FERRY / ASN / 1962 – 1981
1962 – Ailsa Shipyard, Troon, UK

The *Doric Ferry* was ordered by the Atlantic Steam Navigation Co, and together with her earlier sister, the *Cerdic Ferry*, operated from Larne - first to Preston and subsequently to Cairnryan. ASN was taken over by the European Ferries group in 1971 and operations were merged into their subsidiary Townsend Thoresen. By 1981 the *Doric Ferry* and her sister were surplus to requirements, and were both sold to the Compania Armadora de

Sudamerica, for use on the Adriatic as the freighters *Atlas I* and *Atlas II*. From 1984, they were switched to the lengthy Piraeus to Izmir run, and later saw service on domestic Aegean routes. In 1988, the *Atlas II* was acquired by Cycladic Lines, who deployed her from the secondary Athenian port of Rafina to the northern Cycladic island chain. Purchased by Agoudimos Lines in 1989 and renamed the *Kapetan Alexandros*, she continued on the same route but was rebuilt in 1990 into a full passenger vessel, her accommodation being extended aft over her open freight deck. Although cabins replaced some original public rooms, her semi-

To sail no more - the laid-up *Georgios Express* awaits her fate alongside the burnt out *Millennium Express II* near Elefsis, February 2003. *(Richard Seville)*

The *Romilda* swings to berth at the Greek island of Sifnos, July 2003. *(Richard Seville)*

The **Kapetan Alexandros A** alongside at Brindisi in July 2004.
(*Richard Seville*)

DRAGON 1967 – 1986
Ionic Ferry 1986 - 1992
1967 - Ateliers et Chantiers de Bretagne, Nantes, France

The *Dragon* launched Normandy Ferries' route from Southampton to Le Havre in 1967, soon to be joined by her twin sister, the *Leopard*. She remained on this service until the entire Normandy Ferries operation was acquired by Townsend Thoresen in 1985, when her UK port was moved to Portsmouth. In 1986, she was transferred to the Cairnryan to Larne link, receiving the traditional name *Ionic Ferry*. She returned to the P&O fold early in 1987, when her former owners took over Townsend Thoresen's parent company, the European Ferries Group. In October 1987, the firm was rebranded as P&O European Ferries. She continued at

circular lounge bar remains in situ, as do all of her attractive, wooden-panelled and furnished cabins. Agoudimos Lines replaced her at Rafina with the former Sealink vessel *Horsa* (q.v.) in 1992, and she was moved to the Adriatic to serve between Brindisi and Igoumenitsa. She served throughout the 1990s until displaced in 1999 by one-time Townsend Thoresen fleet mate, the rebuilt former *European Gateway* (q.v.). Initially laid-up, the vessel was re-activated in 2001 and, with a slight name change to *Kapetan Alexandros A*, was put into service between Bari and the Albanian port of Durres. In 2004, her 42nd year, she was moved to start operations from Brindisi to Valona, where, backed by intense local marketing, she soon became the premier vessel.

The **Dragon** arrives at Portsmouth in Townsend Thoresen livery during her short spell on the Portsmouth-Le Havre service prior to being transferred to the Irish Sea. (*Miles Cowsill*)

The forlorn **Millennium Express II** at Elefsis, February 2003. *(Richard Seville)*

Cairnryan until 1992, when sold to Marlines for Adriatic service as the *Viscountess M*, where she was again re-united with her sister. With Marlines in steep decline due to more modern competition, she was sold in 1998 to become the *Memed Abashidze* of Gesco Line, for use on the lengthy route from Venice to the Georgian port of Batumi, earning a notorious reputation for poor standards. She passed to Access Ferries in 2000, serving first Igoumenitsa and then Cesme from Brindisi. In 2002 she was due to commence operations to Albania, but whilst on her positioning voyage from Piraeus, she caught fire and burnt out. The gutted hulk was sent to Elefsis, where she lingered alongside the *Georgios Express* (q.v) until towed away for scrapping in April 2003.

EARL GRANVILLE 1980 – 1990
1973 - Jos. L. Meyer, Papenburg, Germany

The *Earl Granville* was built in 1973 as the *Viking 4*, the fifth vessel in the famous Papenburg series delivered to Viking Line. After spending her first seven years on their network linking Sweden and Finland she was sold to Sealink for use between Portsmouth and the Channel Islands. In 1985, following the privatisation of Sealink and sale to Sea Containers, a new deluxe service was launched, under the Starliner and Bateau de Luxe brands. The *Earl Granville* was dispatched for comprehensive refurbishment, emerging with luxurious new interiors. The failure of this concept and the subsequent Channel Islands fiasco is well documented, and the *Earl Granville* finished her UK career serving between Portsmouth and Cherbourg. When the majority of Sealink British Ferries was sold to Stena Line in May 1990, the *Earl Granville* was excluded and retained by Sea Containers. Their plans to transfer her to the Gulf of Mexico for casino cruises fell through, however, as did a proposed sale to Mercandia for charter to Bornholmstraffiken. She was instead sold to Agapitos Bros of Greece becoming their *Express Olympia*. In 1992, the brothers behind this family firm fell out and the fleet was divided – the *Express Olympia* joining newly formed Agapitos Express Ferries. Deployed on the competitive Piraeus to Paros, Naxos and Santorini run, she remained on this route – through both the Agapitos Bros split and the Hellas Ferries take-over in 1999 - until moved to the Piraeus to Samos and Ikaria connection in 2001. She unfortunately developed a rather notorious reputation, with several high-profile incidents blighting

The *Earl Granville* swings off the berth at Portsmouth outward bound to Cherbourg. *(Miles Cowsill)*

The *Express Olympia* captured in the morning sun at Piraeus harbour. *(Miles Cowsill)*

EARL GODWIN 1975 - 1990
1966 - Ab Oresundvarvet, Landskrona, Sweden

If she continues in service throughout 2005, the *Moby Baby* will have spent the same about of time in Moby Lines colours as she did with Sealink. She had been built in 1966 as the *Svea Drott* for use on the overnight service between Helsingborg and Travemunde, but was chartered in 1974 by Sealink to replace the *Falaise* on the Channel Islands route. Purchased at the end of the season and renamed the *Earl Godwin*, she was converted to a day-ship by stripping out all the cabins on her main deck. She remained in service, principally from Weymouth, until the Channel Island Ferries fiasco in 1986, which saw Sealink banned from operating to the islands. For the remainder of her UK career

The *Earl Godwin* leaves St. Helier outward bound for Weymouth in 1986. *(Miles Cowsill)*

her career, including overloading and mechanical breakdowns. Although a far cry from her luxurious Starliner service, her interior remained remarkably unchanged from that era – with all the facilities retaining their Channel Island-themed names and decor. Hence the restaurant was still the Carteret Restaurant, with vignettes of English Earls lining the bulkheads, whilst the midships was the Lily Langtry Lounge, with numerous paintings of the Jersey showgirl on display. Crockery bearing the Sealink logo was also still in active use in the cafeteria! Withdrawn from service after the 2004 season she sold for scrap in spring 2005, leaving Piraeus as the *Express O*.

The colourful **Moby Baby** arriving at Piombino in September 2004. *(Richard Seville)*

she alternated between sporadic service to Cherbourg and lay-up. In early 1990 she was sold to Moby Lines, and introduced on their route from the industrial port of Piombino to the attractive island harbour of Portaferraio on Elba. For a number of years her hull carried a tailored version of Moby's famous whale to suit her name – it was sucking a dummy! In 1998, she became the second of Moby's fleet to receive a full, all-over hull scheme - in her case, colourful shoals of fish created by the famous Italian designer, Ettore Sottsass Jnr. Under Moby's ownership, she has been extensively refitted internally, although traditional BR-style high-backed seating can still be found on board.

EUROMANTIQUE 1995 - 1996
1976 - Framnäs Mek. Verksted, Sandefjord, Norway

Whilst it is common for former UK vessels to be sold to the Mediterranean for further service, moves in the opposite direction are extremely rare. It was therefore highly unusual when two Greek-owned vessels were brought into service by Eurolink, the company formed to re-establish the Sheerness to Vlissingen route after Olau Line's demise. The *Euromantique* had started life as the *Union Hobart*, a freighter built for New Zealand's Union Shipping. She had become the *Seaway Hobart* in 1984, but continued in service until 1993 when acquired by AK Ventouris and brought to Greece for reconstruction. With her

The **Euromantique** was one of a pair of basic ro-pax vessels which Eurolink hoped would replace the luxury Olau Line service between Sheerness and Vlissingen. *(John Hendy collection)*

NEL Lines' *Taxiarchis* pictured at Piraeus, October 2002. *(Richard Seville)*

EUROPIC FERRY 1967 – 1992
European Freighter 1992 - 1993
1967 - Swan Hunter Ltd, Newcastle-upon-Tyne, UK

The *Europic Ferry* was the last vessel built for the Atlantic Steam Navigation Co – debuting in 1967, she was the final evolution of their distinctive freighter design. Deployed from Felixtowe to Rotterdam, she continued on this route after the Townsend Thoresen takeover in 1971. She then moved to Southampton in 1981 and the following year she was requisitioned as part of the Falkland Islands Task Force, sailing to the South Atlantic carrying troops, vehicles, ammunition and stores. From 1983 she was transferred to the Larne to Cairnryan route and in 1984 was converted to carry additional passenger traffic. Operations were re-branded as P&O European Ferries in 1987, but there was little

superstructure extended and passenger accommodation added, she became the *Agia Methodia* and was deployed in traffic across the Adriatic. The charter to Eurolink commenced in April 1995, together with another AK Ventouris fleetmate, the *Attika* which was renamed the *Euromagique*. Sadly, with their limited facilities and awkward layouts, the vessels were not successful and the service closed in late 1996. After a brief charter to Spanish operator Isnasa, the *Euromantique* passed to NEL Lines, where she appears to have found her niche. As the *Taxiarchis*, she serves as back-up to NEL's two major passenger vessels on their links from Piraeus to Chios and Mytilene. If passengers look closely, they can still find the Eurolink logo in evidence on board.

The *Europic Ferry* is seen here inward bound to Southampton following her extensive refit after the Falklands War. *(Miles Cowsill)*

The *Afrodite II* moored at Patras, April 2002. *(Richard Seville)*

impact on the *Europic Ferry* aside from a livery change. Displaced back to a freight role in 1992, she was renamed the *European Freighter* but was sold in 1993 to the newly formed Med Link Lines of Greece. They renamed her the *Afrodite II* and rebuilt her, extending the passenger accommodation aft over her open freight deck. She inaugurated their new operation between Patras and Brindisi offering a full passenger service but with an emphasis on freight and camp-on-board traffic. The route flourished and her accommodation was subsequently extended again. In her final year on the Adriatic, the on board experience was mixed – excellent food and service, but poor maintenance and seeming mechanical problems. There was a clear distinction between the old and new facilities, with the original saloons largely unaltered and the forward lounge bar retaining its elegant wooden-panelling. At the end of the 2002 season, she was withdrawn and laid-up and was finally sold in late 2003 to Ajman Trading. As the *Ajman Glory* it was presumed that she was destined for the scrap yard but incredibly was instead deployed between India and Iraq. However in 2005 she was finally scrapped at Along after only a short period in the Middle East.

A rather sad sight: The *European Gateway* is lifted off the sea-bed off Felixstowe. *(Miles Cowsill collection)*

EUROPEAN GATEWAY 1975 – 1983

1975 - Schichau Unterweser AG, Bremerhaven, Germany

The *European Gateway* was the lead ship of a quartet of highly-successful freighters built for Townsend Thoresen. Her career was cut tragically short when she was involved in a collision with Sealink's *Speedlink Vanguard* off Harwich on 19th December 1982. Having been hit amidships, the *European Gateway* capsized, with the loss of 6 lives from the 70 people on board. When eventually raised in February 1983, most of her superstructure had been washed away, but the hulk was sold to Greek interests who dramatically rebuilt her at Perama. In 1984, she entered Adriatic service as Anco Ferries' *Flavia*. In 1987, B&I Line considered her for

their Rosslare to Pembroke Dock service, but when word leaked of her history, these plans were abandoned. She did however return to northern Europe in 1988 when she was sold to GT Link and deployed between Gedser and Travemunde as the *Travemunde Link 1* – though the '1' was quickly dropped. She was again substantially rebuilt to become a passenger vessel, but in 1991 GT Link failed and she was laid-up. The service was resurrected by Europa Linien in 1992, but she was renamed *Rostock Link* to reflect a change in her German terminal. DSB took over the company in 1996, and by 1998 she had been replaced and moved to Scandlines' Arhus to Liepaja freight route. Subsequently chartered to Mols Linien, she was sold to Agoudimos Lines in 1999 and put in service between Brindisi and Igoumenitsa. The acquisition of the new *Ionian Sky* saw her briefly transferred to Agoudimos' Albanian services, but

The *Penelope A* in early morning sun at Igoumenitsa, July 2003. *(Richard Seville)*

2005 finds her serving Aegean Islands from Thessaloniki. Fascinatingly, much of her crockery bears the Sealink British Ferries logo – having been transferred from her Agoudimos fleetmate, the former *Horsa* (q.v.).

FANTASIA 1990 – 1991
Stena Fantasia 1991 – 1998
P&OSL Canterbury 1998 – 2003
PO Canterbury 2003 – 2003
1980 - Kockums Varv Ab, Malmö, Sweden

The *Fantasia* started life as the deep-sea ro-ro *Scandinavia*. After spending much of the 1980s on long-distance Mediterranean services, she was acquired by Sealink British Ferries in 1988 for conversion into their new flagship for the Dover to Calais run. Initially renamed the *Fiesta*, she swapped names with her French-owned sister prior to entering service. When she debuted in 1990, the vessel brought tremendous innovation to the Channel - with full-length picture windows throughout, a domed discotheque, sweeping staircases, and a two-tier Motorists' Lounge she set new standards across the board. With the *Fiesta*, she became instantly recognisable through her distinctive profile. The *Fantasia* wore no less than six different liveries and four different names during her thirteen years at Dover. Replaced by the new *Pride of Canterbury* in May 2003, another freighter conversion, she was laid up in Dunkirk. Although sold to GA Ferries relatively quickly, she remained in Dunkirk until March 2004. Renamed the *Alkmini A* she was hastily refitted before inaugurating a new route for the

The *Fiesta* undergoing conversion at Lloyd-Werft in Bremerhaven prior to taking up the Dover – Calais service as the *Fantasia*. *(John Hendy)*

The *Stena Fantasia* underwent a series of major and retrograde internal changes after Sealink was absorbed by Stena Line. *(John Hendy)*

Greek operator from Brindisi to Igoumenitsa. Little had changed on board – although her former shopping complex became a recliner lounge. Nonetheless, in the bright Mediterranean, her airy interior came into its own, and she again brought new standards to her route. Her time on the Adriatic was very brief however, for in September 2004 she was re-sold to Polferries for whom she operates as the *Wawel* from Ystad to Swinousjie. Her GA Ferries name has beene cascaded to their latest acquisition, her former fleet mate, the *Pride of Provence*.

The *Alkmini A* pushes away from her berth at Brindisi during July 2004. *(Richard Seville)*

The *Pride of Canterbury* makes a fine sight at speed leaving Boulogne for Dover. *(Miles Cowsill)*

The former *Free Enterprise VIII* is seen here as the *Romilda* swinging off the berth at Paros. *(Miles Cowsill)*

FREE ENTERPRISE VIII 1974 – 1987
Pride of Canterbury 1987 - 1993
1974 - Verolme Dockyard BV, Schiedam, Holland

The eighth and final Free Enterprise-class vessel, the *Free Enterprise VIII* entered service for Townsend Thoresen in 1974. Based at Dover, she served principally on the Zeebrugge link until transferred permanently to the Boulogne service in 1987. With the creation of P&O European Ferries, she was renamed the *Pride of Canterbury* and refitted internally in their corporate style. When the Boulogne route was closed suddenly in January 1993, she was quickly sold to GA Ferries of Greece, becoming their second *Romilda* and displacing the original – formerly her Boulogne competitor, Sealink's *Hengist*. She

was heavily rebuilt, with considerably extended superstructure aft, the latter containing a two-tier reception hall linked by an imposing staircase. She also received a new bow and additional cabins were built into her former hallway on Deck 6. Although initially deployed on the Adriatic between Italy and Greece, GA Ferries withdrew from international trades after the 1993 season and she was moved to the domestic market from Piraeus where she has remained. Her exact route has changed almost constantly, but in recent years she has usually served the Cyclades. Internally, the difference between her original and extended accommodation is distinct - even over a decade later, much P&O branding, signage and even fittings remain in evidence throughout her original facilities.

GALLOWAY PRINCESS 1980 – 1991
Stena Galloway 1991 – 2002
1980 - Harland & Wolff, Belfast, UK

The *Galloway Princess* was the first of the so-called 'Saint' quartet, to which the *St Anselm* (q.v.) and *St Christopher* (q.v) also belong. Delivered in 1980 to Sealink for their Stranraer to Larne run, she remained on the crossing until 1995, when the Irish terminal was switched to Belfast. By this time she was been renamed the *Stena Galloway* following the Stena Line takeover in 1990. She was sold in late 2002 to IMTC of Morocco and renamed *Le Rif*, after the Moroccan mountain range. Although IMTC had previously operated from Tangier to Cadiz, the *Le Rif* was deployed on the shorter Tangier to Algeciras crossing. Operations on this busy

IMTC's *Le Rif* seen at Tangier in May 2003. *(Richard Seville)*

route are run as a pool between no less than seven companies, and although IMTC were initially blocked from joining, they eventually gained entry into this pool. The *Le Rif* hence operates in conjunction with her half-sister, the *St Christopher*, now Limadet's *Ibn Batouta*. Little has changed on board the *Le Rif* since her final Stena Line days, although the former children's play area is now a mosque. Stena Line trim and signage abounds – even Stena Line menus remain in the restaurant. Sadly, their high maintenance standards have not been continued, and even by spring 2003, cockroaches could be seen in the former Globetrotter Cafeteria.

The *Galloway Princess* slowly manoeuvres up to the berth at Stranraer. *(Miles Cowsill)*

GOTLAND 1988 – 1988
1973 - J.L Mosor Brodogradiliste, Trogir, Yugoslavia

The *Gotland* was the second of two overnight ferries delivered to Rederi AB Gotland for services to their home island in 1972/3. Gotland traffic is highly seasonal, however, and as two major vessels would not be required to handle off-peak traffic, the *Gotland* was designed with a dual cruising role in mind and equipped with additional facilities such as an open-air pool. She remained in service with Rederi AB Gotland until they lost the concession to serve the island from 1988 – although ironically she had never actually been used in her intended cruising role. Redundant, she was put on the charter market and after two short-term stints with Mols Linien and Belfast Car Ferries, she was taken on by Brittany Ferries as the second ship on their

In 1989 Brittany Ferries chartered the *Gotland* for additional capacity on their Caen-Portsmouth service. *(Miles Cowsill)*

The heavily rebuilt *Corsica Victoria* unloading at Civitavecchia in September 2004. *(Richard Seville)*

successful Caen to Portsmouth route. As the *Duc de Normandie* was a later derivation of the same Knud.E.Hansen design, the *Gotland* made an ideal running mate. It was initially planned to rename the ship the *Lisieux*, but this never materialised. Despite her compatibility and popularity, the charter was not renewed as Brittany Ferries had the *Prince of Brittany* available for the 1989 season and the *Gotland* was laid up after two further short charters - again to Belfast Car Ferries and then to Sealink Dieppe Ferries. She was sold in early 1989 to Tourship-owned Corsica Ferries, joining her sister, the *Visby*, which had been acquired in 1986. Renamed the *Corsica Victoria*, the former *Gotland* was heavily rebuilt and lengthened over winter 1989/90, emerging with two additional cabin decks above her original structure and a dramatic new profile. Since her acquisition, the *Corsica Victoria*

The *Horsa* coming astern into Folkestone towards the end of her railway ownership in 1984. *(John Hendy)*

has been deployed on a variety of routes between Italy, France, Corsica and Sardinia but for 2004 partnered the *Sardinia Nova* on the 8-hour Civitavecchia to Golfo Aranchi crossing.

HORSA 1972 – 1990
Stena Horsa 1990 - 1992
1972 - Arsenal de la Marine National Francaise, Brest, France

Together with her sister, the *Hengist*, the *Horsa* remains an icon of Sealink's much-lamented Folkestone to Boulogne route. Having brought drive through services to the crossing when delivered in 1972, the *Horsa* remained on the link through privatisation until

the 1990 season when briefly transferred to Holyhead. With the acquisition of Sealink by Stena Line in the same year, however, she was recalled to Folkestone, gained the Stena prefix to her name, and ultimately became the ship that closed the route on 31st December 1991. Sold to Agoudimos Lines of Greece to become their *Penelope A*, she entered service as the company's flagship on their route from Rafina to the northern Cycladic islands of Andros, Tinos and Mykonos. Early in her Greek career her superstructure was extended aft to provide a spacious deck shelter and her side promenades were glassed-in. Renamed the *Express Penelope* when Agoudimos' domestic services were absorbed into the expanding Hellas Ferries operation in late 1999, she returned to her original Greek owners and name in early 2004, still serving on the same route. Internally, although now a two-class vessel, she remains very much the *Stena Horsa*, complete with The Pantry cafeteria and the famous VSOE, or Orient Express Lounge, installed in 1986 and still offering dark-wood-effect panelling and faux gold trim.

The handsome *Penelope A* at her berth in Mykonos, July 2004. *(Richard Seville)*

INNISFALLEN 1969 – 1980
Spirit of Independence 1995 - 1995
1969 - Werft Nobiskrug GmbH, Rendsburg, Germany

The *Derin Deniz* is well known in the UK for two very different operations – firstly as B+I's *Innisfallen*, and later as Meridian Ferries' unfortunate *Spirit of Independence*. Having served the Irish firm until 1980, principally from Cork to Swansea, she was sold to Corsica Ferries becoming the *Corsica Viva*. After five years on their core routes from Italy to Corsica, she was moved to the Caribbean to launch an innovative new venture linking Puerto Rico and the Dominican Republic, under the name *Dominican Viva*. This operation failed and by 1988 she was back in the Mediterranean

under the name *Corsica Viva 1*. Having become the *Sardinia Viva* in 1992, she returned back to the Caribbean in 1993 as the *Caribia Viva*, seemingly for another Tourship venture, Caribia Ferries. 1994 found her chartered to various Mediterranean operators before passing to Meridian Ferries to launch passenger services from Folkestone to Boulogne. Sadly, their admirable attempts were frustrated by the actions of striking French seamen, who even managed to set fire to one of the vessel's lounges whilst alongside. Meridian Ferries subsequently collapsed and she was moved to La Spezia for lay-up. It was not until 1998 that she was re-activated to become the *Happy Dolphin* for short-lived Happy Lines. In 2001 she was arrested and laid up again, eventually being sold to Sancak Lines of Turkey in 2003 and renamed *Derin Deniz*, purportedly for use in

The *Innisfallen* turns off the Cleddau Bridge to approach the berth at Pembroke Dock. *(Miles Cowsill)*

The distinctive looking **Black Watch** at speed in the English Channel. *(FotoFlite)*

the Black Sea. However, with the loss of their flagship, the *Sancak 1* (formerly Swedish Lloyd's first *Saga* of 1966), she instead debuted on their main route from Brindisi to Cesme. Their permanent plans for her evidently were never realised for in late 2004 she was beached at Alang for breaking. (see page 26 for comparative photo)

JUPITER 1966 – 1990
Black Watch 1966 - 1986
1966 – Flender Werft, Lubeck, Germany

The *Jupiter* was constructed for Fred. Olsen and Bergen Line for an innovative dual role. Along with a twin sister, the *Venus*, she would alternate between summer months operating on North Sea ferry services and winter employment sailing as a passenger-cargo liner to the Canaries under the name *Black Watch*. From 1981, the North Sea services were operated by DFDS Seaways, although she was never painted in their colours and the winter-time arrangement continued. In 1986 she passed to the recently formed Norway Line, who had taken over the former Fred Olsen route the previous year. She then commenced full-time service from Newcastle to Bergen until replaced by a new *Venus* (q.v) in 1990. Acquired by Marlines for their booming Italy to Greece

The sunlit **Byblos** laid up at anchor in Elefsis Bay, February 2003. *(Richard Seville)*

The **Norris Castle** leaving Cowes for Southampton following her stretching in 1976. *(John Hendy)*

routes and renamed the *Crown M*, in early years her voyages continued as far as Heraklion and even Limassol. Unlike her Marlines fleet-mates, she was not rebuilt at all, and to this day retains her handsome original profile. Marlines however struggled to compete with the purpose-built competition which emerged from the mid-1990s, and in 1997 the *Crown M* was withdrawn and laid up in Elefsis Bay. Sold to Lebanese interests in 2000 and renamed *Byblos*, she has none-the-less remained in her Marlines colours. Reactivated for short-term hotel-ship use in July 2001, she has otherwise remained at anchor in an increasingly-empty Elefsis Bay, spending 2003 lashed to the Belgian veteran *Express Hermes*, formerly RMT's *Princesse Astrid*. Although seemingly well maintained, a return to service appears increasingly unlikely.

NORRIS CASTLE 1968 - 1994
1968 – J. I. Thornycroft & Co. Ltd., Southampton, UK

Built as a bow-only loading car ferry for Red Funnel for their hour-long domestic route from Southampton to Cowes, the *Norris Castle* underwent substantial surgery in 1976 to convert her for drive-through operations. She emerged with a significantly altered profile and an additional passenger saloon, and went on to serve on the Solent until replaced by the new *Red Osprey* in 1994. She was rapidly acquired by Jadrolinija to serve their extensive network of routes in the beautiful Croatian archipelago. Although initially envisaged only to remain in service for five years, she continues in operation today, together with her

The **Lovrjenac** bathed in late afternoon sun whilst leaving Split, July 2003. *(Richard Seville)*

Red Funnel fleetmates, the *Nehaj*, ex-*Cowes Castle* and the *Sis*, ex *Netley Castle*. Indeed, remarkably, all of Red Funnel's purpose-built car ferries remain in active service – the 1959-built *Carisbrooke Castle* in Italy and the 1962-built *Osborne Castle* in Canada. Although Jadrolinija's fleet deployment changes frequently, in recent years the *Lovrjenac* has been based in Split, predominantly serving the hour-long crossing to Rogac on the island of Solta. Her interior remains essentially unaltered.

NORSTAR 1974 - 2001
1974 - AG Weser, Bremerhaven, Germany

The *SNAV Campania* was built as the Dutch-flagged *Norstar* for North Sea Ferries booming Hull to Rotterdam route. Together with her sister, the Falklands-veteran *Norland*, she was stretched in 1987 prior to transfer to the Zeebrugge route, which she served until displacement in 2001. The sisters were sold as a pair to fast-

Two former Folkestone vessels pass each other in Piraeus harbour. The former *Vortigern*, seen here as the *Express Milos*, passes the *Express Santorini* (ex. *Chartres*) in September 2002. *(Miles Cowsill)*

The **Nisos Limnos** heads out of Syros in her final season, July 2004. *(Richard Seville)*

craft operator SNAV, who wanted to launch a new conventional route from Naples to Palermo. Renamed the *SNAV Campania* after the region in which Naples is situated, the former *Norstar* has been transferred to the British register and retains Hull as her home port today. Her pattern of services is identical to when with North Sea Ferries, as she makes just one overnight trip per day. Internally, the vessel remains virtually unaltered – the only significant change is the conversion of two of her shops into a games arcade and a TV lounge. Surprisingly no separate formal restaurant has been created, instead the vast buffet restaurant simply serves as a self-service cafeteria. Externally, the vessels have been shot-blasted and are immaculately maintained. The most striking changes on board however are the alterations made due to the new ISPS legislation. Unlike many operators, SNAV

The SNAV *Campania* glistens in early morning sunlight at Palermo, Sicily, September 2004. *(Richard Seville)*

have acted immediately to fulfil all requirements, and full-size iron gates now block entry to all crew areas as well as the car decks.

OLAU WEST 1975 - 1977
1964 - Unterweser A.G., Bremerhaven, Germany

The *Azzurra's* stay in UK waters was limited to three years, but she was none-the-less a pivotal vessel – for, as the *Olau West*, she inaugurated Olau Line's passenger services. She had been built for Danish internal service as the *Grenaa*, together with a sister, the *Hundsted*. Both ships were acquired by the fledgling Olau Line in late 1974, and as the *Olau East* and *Olau West* established

North Sea Ferries' vessel *Norstar* swings in the inner harbour at Hull outward bound to Zeebrugge. *(Miles Cowsill)*

The **Olau West** laid the foundations for Olau Line's successful Sheerness – Vlissingen service. *(John Hendy collection)*

Azzurra, she has been comprehensively refitted, and – on the surface – boasts a bright, modern interior. Indications are, however, that she is not well mechanically, and the erratic nature of her deployment suggests she may be struggling to compete – her exact deployment has changed every year, with a variety of new routes being tried and then abandoned. Nonetheless, sailing into her 41st year, she is a remarkable survivor.

PRINCE LAURENT 1974 – 1990
1974 - Boelwerf, Temse, Belgium

The *Prince Laurent* was delivered to RMT in 1974, a sister to the earlier *Prins Philippe* of 1973. She served the Belgians through their alliance changes in the 1980s – sailing in both Sealink and Townsend

passenger operations in January 1975. The *Olau East* was sold to Venezuela the same year, but the *Olau West* remained in the fleet until 1977. During her final season, she launched the ill-fated Sheerness to Dunkirk route, and was sold in an attempt to re-coup some the losses incurred. She subsequently spent thirteen years with Corsica Ferries as the *Corsica Marina*, until sold in 1990 to Alimar to become their *Kelibia*. From 1995, she entered a nomadic phase when used on a number of unsuccessful services under a succession of different operators and names. When laid-up in 2000, at 36 years of age, the scrap yard must surely have beckoned but against the odds she was acquired by yet another start-up company – the Adriatic Shipping Company. As their

The **Azzurra** turning to berth at Dubrovnik in July 2003. *(Richard Seville)*

Hellas Ferries' *Express Poseidon* (ex *St. Patrick*) is seen here at the berth pending her morning departure into the Aegean. *(Miles Cowsill)*

The former Townsend Thoresen vessel *Viking Viscount* swings off the berth at the Crete port of Agios Nikolaoes. *(Miles Cowsill)*

Thoresen colours, along with a modified version of P&O European Ferries livery and then the dedicated Dover - Ostend Line scheme. Replaced by the new *Prins Filip* in 1992, the *Prince Laurent* was rapidly sold to Strintzis Lines of Greece and left Ostend as the *Ionian Express*. She was radically rebuilt at Perama, during which she gained a new bow and was extended at the stern. Before completion, she was again renamed, becoming the *Superferry II* as she was to replace the original *Superferry* on Strintzis' Rafina to Andros, Tinos and Mykonos route. Her interior had been transformed into a modern, open-plan design, with a coffee bar instead of a full self-service. The upper forward lounge was segregated to create a new Distinguished-Class area, as is standard in Greek domestic service. In 1999, the Attika group acquired a majority shareholding in Strintzis Lines, and

The *Superferry II* storms into Andros in July 2004. *(Richard Seville)*

operations were restyled as Blue Star Ferries. Initially, the *Superferry II* operated under the Blue Ferries brand that was applied to the firm's older vessels, but since 2003 has appeared in full Blue Star livery. She continues to serve her original Greek route, regularly encountering her sister, which now sails as Hellenic Seaways' *Express Athina*.

PRINSES MARIA-ESMERALDA 1975 – 1995
1975 - Cockerill, Hoboken, Belgium

The *Prinses Maria-Esmeralda* was the lead ship in a trio of multi-purpose ferries commissioned by RMT in the mid to late 1970s,

RMT's *Prince Laurent* leaves Dover Western Docks on a train-connected service for Ostend. *(John Hendy)*

The ***Prinses Maria-Esmeralda*** on a morning sailing between Ostend and Dover Eastern Docks. Following the break with Sealink in 1976, the vessel's trading name was removed before she adopted the Townsend Thoresen orange hull. *(John Hendy)*

The ***Beni Ansar*** approaching Nador in August 2002. *(Richard Seville)*

all of which were unattractively jumboised in 1985/6. While her sisters still serve Ostend for TransEuropa Ferries, the *Prinses Maria-Esmeralda* has had a much more varied career. Rendered redundant together with the *Prince Laurent* (q.v.) in 1992, she languished in Ostend for three years on the sales list until acquired by the then-unknown company Denval Marine. Denval are the operator behind TransEuropa Ferries, which at that stage only had operations in the Adriatic. Renamed *Wisteria*, the former 'PME' sporadically operated for TEF interspersed with periods on charter, including a spell with Limadet in 1997 when she was temporarily renamed the *Beni Ansar*. After a further charter to Limadet in 1999, she was ultimately sold to the

Moroccan company in 2000, and, again renamed the *Beni Ansar*, has since been the mainstay of their Almeria to Nador route. Since sale from RMT, she has had additional cabins built into lounge space and her former upper vehicle garage.

PRINZ HAMLET 1973 – 1986
Prins Hamlet 1986 – 1988
1973 - Werft Nobiskrug GmbH, Rendsburg, Germany

The *Prinz Hamlet* started life operating for German Prinzen Linien from Harwich to Hamburg. Prinzen Linien were taken over by DFDS Seaways in 1981, but her operations remained little changed,

The **Azzurra** turning to berth at Dubrovnik in July 2003. *(Richard Seville)*

The elegant *Ancona* berthed at the Croatian port of Split in July 2003. *(Richard Seville)*

The **Prince Hamlet** was chartered to B&I Ferries to maintain their Rosslare service in 1987. *(Miles Cowsill)*

The **Sveti Stefan** loading in Ancona during June 2004. *(Richard Seville)*

although in 1986 her name was amended to the Danish spelling of 'Prins'. She was replaced by the *Hamburg* in 1987, and after briefly serving from Newcastle, was sold to Stena Line in 1988. Her purchase was a shrewd investment move for Stena, who rapidly resold her to Polferries without ever having employed her themselves. As the *Nieborow* she saw service on all their routes until sold in 2002 to Prekoanska Plovidba, trading as Montenegro Lines. Since re-establishing operations in 1998 with the former Brittany Ferries vessel *Cornauailles*, Montenegro Lines have steadily grown and acquired the *Nieborow* to initiate a new route between Bar and Ancona. Renamed the *Sveti Stefan II* after the famous Montenegrin landmark, the former *Prinz Hamlet* also provides additional capacity on their original Bar to Bari link. The vessel's interior is unaltered from her Polferries' days – right down to advertisements for duty-free shopping in Sweden!

ROI BAUDOUIN 1965 - 1983
1965 - Cockerill, Hoboken, Belgium

The *Roi Baudouin* must surely rate as one of the most elegant vessels ever to serve UK waters. Commissioned in 1965 for the Belgian Marine Administration (later RMT), she sailed from Ostend to Dover for 18 years until laid up and offered for sale in late 1982. Early the following year she sailed to Greece as the *Georgios B*, having been sold to Ventouris Ferries. Prior to entering service she was rebuilt astern with larger sun decks and renamed again, this time to *Georgios Express*. She entered service from Piraeus to the Cyclades, principally serving the central trunk down to Santorini. When the Ventouris family's operations were split up with the retirement of patriarch Konstantinos Ventouris, she passed to Vangelis Ventouris who founded Ventouris Sea Lines. 1995 saw

The handsome Belgian Marine car ferry **Roi Baudouin** of 1965 leaving Ostend for her afternoon sailing to Harwich in 1968. *(John Hendy)*

The **Georgios Express** laid up at Elefsis, February 2003. *(Richard Seville)*

the dramatic financial collapse of VSL and she was laid up in Piraeus' Great Harbour, where she was to languish for four years. The final vessel in the fleet to find new employment, it was not until 1999 that she was re-activated. Under Ventouris control, she was deployed on a complicated timetable of Cycladic services based in Syros, wearing an all white-livery, without any company markings except for the VSL funnel logo. Many reminders of her original incarnation remained, including a profile painting of her as the *Roi Baudouin*. On board services were minimal, without any catering facilities operating, even on voyages lasting over eight hours. Her return to service was to prove an Indian summer however, for she was confined to port in the wake of the *Express Samina* tragedy in September 2000 and never returned to service. Laid-up at first in Syros, she was later moved to Elefsis where she was sandwiched between the UK veterans *Dragon* and *Hebrides*. Today she remains laid up at an Elefsis shipyard, her future is very uncertain.

SAINT ELOI 1975 – 1989
Channel Entente 1989 – 1990
King Orry 1990 - 1998
1975 - Cantieri Navali di Pietra Ligure, Pietra Ligure, Italy

The *Saint Eloi* is infamous as the vessel that was delivered three years late. A close sister to Sealink UK's *Vortigern* (q.v.), the multi-purpose ferry was ordered from her Italian builders in 1969 for delivery in 1972, but work ceased due to financial problems at the yard and it was not until 1975 that she arrived in Dover. Built to

The *Moby Drea* backs up to her berth at Livorno in September 2004. *(Richard Seville)*

The **Al Mansour** heads out of Algeciras bound for Tangier during May 2003. *(Richard Seville)*

The train ferry **Saint Eloi** in mid-Channel, and sailing from Dunkirk West to Dover, is viewed from the bridge of the **Saint-Germain**. *(John Hendy)*

The **Moby Love** approaching Portaferrio on the Italian island of Elba, September 2004. *(Richard Seville)*

the order of Sealink subsidiary ALA, she was to spend thirteen years on the train ferry route from Dover to Dunkirk until displaced by the new *Nord-Pas-de-Calais* in 1988. She subsequently spent two years operating rail-connected sailings from Dover to Calais firstly for SNCF and then Sealink British Ferries, latterly as the *Channel Entente*. In 1990 she was purchased by the Isle of Man Steam Packet, who were seeking a replacement for the elderly *Tynwald* (q.v.). After proving herself during her first season, the *Channel Entente* was dispatched for transformation into the new flagship, the *King Orry*. Comfortably refitted, she served the island faithfully until 1998 when replaced by the new *Ben-my-Chree*. Moby Lines then acquired her to bolster their fleet on the hour-long shuttle

service between Piombino and Portaferraio on the island of Elba, where she joined former Sealink fleetmate *Earl Godwin* (q.v.). Initially renamed *Moby Love 2*, she has since lost the suffix. Although she has seen peak season service from Piombino to Bastia, recent years have seen her concentrate on the Elba service. Her interior has been comprehensively refitted, although the IOMSP logo can still be found in the snug Kings Head Pub, now in use as a conference room!

SAINT KILLIAN 1978 – 1982
Saint Killian II 1982 – 1998
1973 - Titovo Brodogradiliste, Kraljevica, Yugoslavia

The *Saint Killian* first arrived in UK waters in 1978, when Irish Continental Line (ICL) introduced her onto their services between Ireland and France. She had been built in 1973 as the *Stena Scandinavica* for their overnight route from Gothenburg to Kiel, also seeing service on the short Kiel to Korsor run. In 1982, ICL sent her for lengthening in Amsterdam, from which she returned as the *Saint Killian II*. She continued in service until 1997, by which time ICL had been renamed Irish Ferries. After over a year laid up, she was sold to Greek interests and headed to Piraeus as the *Medina Star*. However, she was destined to remain inactive for another four years, languishing in Elefsis Bay as plans for her new career failed. In 2002 she was acquired by Hellenic Mediterranean Lines and a comprehensive refurbishment began. Renamed the *Egnatia III*, she finally entered service on their route from Patras to Brindisi, often via Igoumenitsa and the Ionian Islands, in summer 2003. HML had completely revitalised her interior and she offered bright and comfortable facilities, filled with HML memorabilia. Unfortunately, HML have long been in decline and for 2004 she was chartered to Algerie Ferries for use between Marseille and Algeria. HML meanwhile faced a disastrous season after their remaining vessel, the *Poseidonia* (q.v.) broke down. By the time the *Egnatia III* returned from charter, their future was in serious doubt. HML have not themselves offered a service in 2005, and the *Egnatia III* remains inactive in Elefis Bay, still in Algerie Ferries colours.

The *Egnatia III* berthed at Patras during July 2003, her only season of service for HML. *(Richard Seville)*

The *St. Killian II* is seen here outward bound to Cherbourg from Rosslare during her last season. *(Miles Cowsill)*

SAINT PATRICK 1973 – 1982
Saint Columb 1982 – 1982
Saint Colum 1 1982 - 1990
1973 - Unterweser AG, Bremerhaven, Germany

As the *Saint Patrick*, the *Express Poseidon* inaugurated Irish Continental Lines services between Ireland and France. The new operation prospered, and by 1982 she was replaced by larger tonnage and moved to launch a new subsidiary resurrecting the former P&O route between Liverpool and Belfast. Her new name of *Saint Columb* was quickly amended to *Saint Colum 1* to avoid confusion with Sealink's *St Columba*. Interestingly, her bell still displays the name *Saint Columb 1* – a name she never actually wore – the '1' having been added without removing the 'b'. Despite regular rumours that new tonnage was being sought, the *Saint Colum 1* closed the route she had started during October 1990, and she was offered for sale. She sailed to Greece to become Arkadia Lines' *Dimitrios Express*, where she was heavily built-up at the stern. A series of tiered sun decks were created astern with a new lido and pool, but her interior was little changed. With a striking new appearance she entered service between Brindisi and Igoumenitsa, but in 1996 was moved to the Aegean at short notice to operate on the lucrative Central Cyclades route from Piraeus. This was to cover for Arkadia's *Poseidon Express*, which had capsized at Paros, and for this new role, the *Dimitrios Express* became the *Poseidon Express 2*. Arkadia's operations diminished in the late 1990s, and by the time they were absorbed into the new Hellas Ferries

The **St. Colum I** reopened the Liverpool-Belfast service in 1982. *(Miles Cowsill collection)*

The **Express Poseidon** arrives at the Greek island of Paros, July 2004. *(Richard Seville)*

conglomerate in 1999, the *Poseidon Express 2* was their only vessel. Renamed *Express Poseidon*, she remained in service 2004, although her appearance was more conservative following the removal of a glass conservatory that initially adorned her bridge. She was sold to Indian breakers in Spring 2005.

SCANDINAVIA 1988 - 1988
Venus 1989 – 1994
King of Scandinavia 1994 – 2002
1974 - Wärtsilä Ab, Åbo, Finland

Commissioned for Sessan Linjen's Gothenburg to Travemunde route, the *Prinsessan Birgitta* came under Stena Line control following their takeover of Sessan in 1981. Renamed *Stena Scandinavica*, her German destination was switched to Kiel, and she continued in service until displaced in 1987 by which time her name had been shortened to *Scandinavia*. She then entered the charter market, serving first Cotunav and then, surprisingly being an overnight vessel, Sealink British Ferries from Dover to Calais for a short time in the summer of 1988. She returned to Cotunav as the *Tarek L* in 1989, before being sold to Norway Line for use on the Newcastle to Bergen / Stavanger route as the *Venus*. Norway Line merged with Jahre Line to form Color Line in 1991, and in 1994 she was exchanged for Scandinavian Seaways' larger *King of Scandinavia*, consequently assuming that name herself. She remained on the Tyne, but her destination

During the P&O strike of 1988, Sealink chartered the **Scandinavia** to operate extra services from Dover to Zeebrugge and Calais. *(John Hendy collection)*

The **Cesme** sunlit at Ancona in the early evening, June 2004. *(Richard Seville)*

The **Moby Vincent** turns to enter the Corsican port of Bastia in June 2002. *(Richard Seville)*

Hellas Ferriesi *Express Apollon* off Andros in July 2004. *(Richard Seville)*

changed to Ijmuiden. Increasingly redundant within the DFDS Seaways' fleet, she saw several charters back to Cotanav, before sale in 2002 to Turkish Marmara Lines. A new entrant in the competitive peak season Italy to Turkey trade, TML renamed her the *Cesme*, and inaugurated services with the Italian destination alternating between Ancona and Brindisi. The company's name has since been shortened to Marmara Lines.

SENLAC 1973 – 1987
1973 - Arsenal de la Marine National Francaise, Brest, France

The third sister of the attractive *Hengist*-class, the *Senlac* was delivered in 1973 for service on Sealink's Newhaven to Dieppe route, jointly operated by British Rail and SNCF. The British contribution to the link, the *Senlac* was to have a relatively short UK career. Following the privatisation of Sealink in 1984, new owners Sea Containers announced their intention to pull out of the joint service. Early in 1985 the *Senlac* was sold to SNCF, but although she initially continued in operation, she was displaced by the newly acquired *Versailles* in 1987. She spent the summer on charter to B&I between Fishguard and Rosslare and it is rumoured that the Irish company belatedly expressed interest in purchasing her – but they were too late, for in November 1987 she was sold to Ventouris Sea Lines (VSL). Renamed the *Apollo Express* she joined their large fleet of ex-UK tonnage serving the Cyclades from Piraeus. She was joined by her sister the *Hengist* as the *Apollo Express 2* from 1993, but VSL encountered severe financial difficulties and collapsed in late 1995. The *Senlac*, by then the

The *Express Apollon* pulls away from Sifnos, July 2003. *(Richard Seville)*

The Newhaven – Dieppe ferry *Senlac* was Sealink's third and final Brest-built vessel and entered service in 1973. *(John Hendy)*

Apollo Express 1, was ultimately sold in 1996 to the expansionist Agapitos Express Ferries for use on the same route with a simple name change to *Express Apollon*. Swallowed up in the mergers that created Hellas Ferries in late 1999, the *Express Apollon* was re-united with both her sisters between 1999 and 2003. Although both have since been sold from the Hellas Ferries fleet, the former *Senlac* remains and will serve the Cyclades again in 2005 under the new Hellenic Seaways brand. Comprehensively refurbished over the years, she is still an extremely comfortable vessel with contemporary interiors – although her heritage is visible through a series of panels depicting the Bayeux Tapestry in her cafeteria and her former name is even still in evidence in the forward stairwell fibre-glass mural by Franta Belsky.

The *Redentore 1* seen at speed en route to Ischia during September 2004. *(Richard Seville)*

SOLIDOR 1977 - 1989
1965 - Jos L. Meyer, Papenburg, Germany

As the original *Solidor*, the former *Langeland* was used to establish Emeraude Lines' Channel Island operations. Built in 1965 for the route from Bagenkop to Kiel, she was sold to Vedettes Blanches in 1977 having been replaced by a larger new build, the *Langeland II*. Principally a local Breton operator, Vedettes Blanches used the new *Solidor* to commence year-round services from St Malo to Jersey, launching the new brand of Emeraude Ferries – subsequently amended to Lines. Just over a decade later she was again replaced by the *Langeland II*, when Emeraude Lines acquired her successor to become the *Solidor II*. The original *Solidor* was then sold to

Emeraude's *Solidor,* seen entering the harbour at St. Helier (Jersey) in 1980, at the conclusion of a morning sailing from St. Malo. *(John Hendy)*

The **Barlovento** arriving at Los Cristianos, Tenerife, in August 2003. *(Richard Seville)*

Local caiques provide an attractive foreground to the *Express Aphrodite* as she arrives at Mykonos, October 2002. *(Richard Seville)*

The **Solidor 3** is shown here during her brief period in Emeraude Lines colours' leaving St Malo. *(Marko Stampehl)*

The **Tangier Jet** powers towards Spain off the Moroccan coast, May 2003. *(Richard Seville)*

Buono, a local Naples operator, to run from Pozzuoli to Ischia as the *Redentore 1*, but in 1992 she was purchased by the Lauro group and absorbed into their new Traghetti Pozzuoli fleet without a change of name. Serving alongside the former *Caledonia* as the *Heidi* and Townsend's former *Autocarrier* as the *Ischia*, the *Redentore 1* carried Traghetti Pozzuoli's bright green and yellow colours until a more conservative black and white scheme was introduced in 2003.

SOLIDOR 3 1996 - 2001
1996 - Kværner Fjellstrand, Omastrand, Norway

The *Solidor 3* was Emeraude Lines' second attempt to introduce a major fast ferry – their first purpose-built vessel, the *Emeraude*, having been withdrawn and sold after just two months in service in

1994. The *Solidor 3* was considerably more successful, serving for five years between St Malo and the Channel Islands until replaced by the larger *Solidor 5* in 2001. She was then sold to FRS Iberia for use between Tarifa and Tangier across the Straits of Gibraltar. FRS, or Forde Reederei Seetouristik are a German firm with extensive ferry interests around Europe. In addition to their original services to Heligoland, they also own the Romo-Sylt Ferry, Nordic Jet Line and FRS Iberia. The purchase of the *Solidor 3*, which was renamed the *Tangier Jet*, was entirely logical as FRS already owned two sister vessels, the *Nordic Jet* and the *Baltic Jet*, which are deployed from Helsinki to Tallinn, but have also seen service for FRS Iberia.

The *Spirit of Free Enterprise* was the lead ship in Townsend Thoresen's trio of ferries for their Dover – Calais 'Blue Riband' service. *(John Hendy)*

SPIRIT OF FREE ENTERPRISE 1980 – 1987
Pride of Kent 1987 – 1998
P&OSL Kent 1998 – 2002
PO Kent 2002 – 2003
1980 - Schichau-Unterweser AG, Bremerhaven, Germany

The *Spirit of Free Enterprise* was delivered to Townsend Thoresen in 1980, the lead ship of a trio ordered for their core Dover to Calais route. Their service speed of 23 knots allowed crossing times to be cut to 75 minutes and the sisters were immediately successful. The class hit notoriety in 1987 when the second vessel, the *Herald of Free Enterprise*, capsized off Zeebrugge, but the remaining two ships have led relatively quiet lives. In the aftermath of her sister's loss,

the Townsend Thoresen brand disappeared in favour of P&O European Ferries, and the *Spirit of Free Enterprise* was renamed the *Pride of Kent*. She continued in service on the Calais run and in 1991 was sent for lengthening in Palermo, Sicily to bring her up to the standards of the latest vessels on the route. Emerging with a bulkier appearance and greatly enlarged passenger accommodation, she was to remain in the P&O fleet until 2003, having been renamed *P&OSL Kent* during the P&O Stena Line era from 1998 and *PO Kent* when P&O bought Stena Line out in 2002. Replaced by the Darwin conversions, she was sold to GA Ferries of Greece for deployment on their main Piraeus to Rhodes route, a voyage of up to 18 hours. Renamed the *Anthi Marina*, she was converted at Perama for her new role, which included remodelling of her bow

The *Anthi Marina* berthed at Piraeus, July 2004. *(Richard Seville)*

Limadet's *Ibn Batouta* leaves the port of Algeciras outward bound to Tangier. *(Miles Cowsill)*

The *Isla de Botafoc* slips out of Barcelona bound for the Ibiza, August 2003. *(Richard Seville)*

and new terraces aft. On board changes are surprisingly limited, however, and contrary to rumour, no new cabins have been installed, with former crew cabins instead opened for public use. Those changes that have been made are seemingly illogical with a vast recliner lounge replacing the former Langan's Restaurant and ro-ro lounge but the shopping complex remaining in its entirety. Most other facilities retain their original function – including the First Base Burger bar – but the Club Lounge is now a private owner's lounge. GA Ferries have also acquired her former Dover fleetmate, the *Pride of Provence*, which has been chartered to Kystlink.

ST ANSELM / Sealink UK / 1980 – 1990
Stena Cambria / Sealink Stena Line / 1990 – 1999
1980 – Harland & Wolff, Belfast, UK

Sealink's *St. Anselm* entered service on the Dover - Calais service in October 1980 in direct competition with Townsend Thoresen's trio. *(John Hendy)*

The second of the so-called 'Saint' quartet built in Belfast, the *St Anselm* was ordered for Sealink's Dover to Calais service. Upon replacement by the *Fantasia* (q.v.) in 1990, she spent a season at Folkestone before moving to support the *Stena Hibernia* at Holyhead as the *Stena Cambria*. She returned to Dover in 1996 to provide additional tonnage following the Stena / SNAT split, before finishing her career in P&O Stena Line colours on the Newhaven to Dieppe run. She was then purchased by Umafisa of Ibiza, a company whose origins lay in local services from Ibiza Town. After a lengthy refit, she launched their service from Ibiza Town to Barcelona. During her conversion, cabins were built into former lounge space and her shopping complex aft on the main deck, whilst reclining seats were added in several other locations. The remainder of her public rooms were left completely unaltered and until 2004 her cafeteria remained in the format of Sealink British Ferries' The Pantry, while elsewhere she retained her Harbour Coffee Co. branding from the P&O Stena Line era. 2003 saw Umafisa taken over by rival Balearia, who absorbed operations into their own fleet, and have since utilised her on a variety of services to the mainland. In 2005 she was underwent a major refurbishment.

Sister ship **St. Christopher** is pictured during 1984 when Sealink was denationalised and her funnel markings were painted out. *(John Hendy)*

ST CHRISTOPHER 1981 – 1990
Stena Antrim 1990 - 1998
1981 – Harland & Wolff, Belfast, UK

The third of Sealink's Belfast-built quartet, the *St Christopher* was constructed for the Dover to Calais route with her sister, the *St Anselm*. When ordered, Sealink anticipated that their Seaspeed business would soon carry the majority of passengers across the Channel and hence the Dover 'Saints" passenger capacity was relatively low. This incorrect assumption saw the twins'

superstructure extended aft in 1983 to increase their capacity. In 1991, the *St Christopher* was transferred to the Stranraer to Larne run as the *Stena Antrim*. The Irish terminal was moved to Belfast in 1995 prior to the arrival of the HSS *Stena Voyager*, which displaced the *Stena Antrim*. Initially laid-up, she was subsequently deployed on the Newhaven to Dieppe route without a change of name. Replaced by her sister, the *Stena Cambria*, in April 1998 she was quickly sold to Limadet of Morocco for use between Tangier and Algeciras as their third *Ibn Batouta*. She was reunited with her half-sister, the *Galloway Princess*, when rival operator acquired the latter

The **Ibn Batouta** arrives at Algeciras during May 2003. *(Richard Seville)*

in 2002 to become their *Le Rif*. On board, the *Ibn Batouta* too retains many reminders of her UK career – both her self-service cafeteria and main bar retain the styling installed by Sealink British Ferries. In order to meet the needs of travellers, the one-time video warp has however been converted into a mosque - although surreally all the associated fluorescent trim remains!

ST COLUMBA 1977 – 1991
Stena Hibernia 1991 – 1996
Stena Adventurer 1996 - 1997
1977 - Aalborg Vaerft, Aalborg, Denmark

Commissioned in 1977 for Sealink's Holyhead to Dun Laoghaire route, the *St Columba* was the mainstay of the service for nearly twenty years. During this period she passed through three different owners and numerous livery changes. British-Rail-owned Sealink was sold to Sea Containers upon denationalisation in 1984 and then just six years later was acquired by Stena Line after a hostile take-over bid. Originally built as a two-class vessel, the *St Columba* became one-class in 1982 and her accommodation later saw two major rebuilds, once in 1986 and then again in 1991 when she was renamed the *Stena Hibernia*. This refit was the first attempt to bring Stena Line's Travel Service Concept to the UK and initially resulted in widespread controversy. In 1996 Stena introduced their new HSS onto the route and the *Stena Hibernia* was relegated to back-up status. In anticipation of a move to the Dover Strait, she was renamed the *Stena Adventurer*, but this move never happened and after a year in support, she was sold in early 1997 to Agapitos Express Ferries. This rapidly expanding company had only been formed in 1992,

The **St. Columba** leaves Fishguard for Rosslare. *(Miles Cowsill)*

but had astutely profited from the demise of rivals Ventouris Sea Lines to swell their fleet – and as the *Express Aphrodite*, the former *St Columba* became their sixth vessel. With two-class accommodation reinstated, she was used to inaugurate a new daytime route from Piraeus to the northern Cycladic island chain, terminating in Mykonos, which was instantly successful. Agapitos Express Ferries were absorbed into the new Hellas Ferries conglomerate in late 1999, but the *Express Aphrodite's* operations initially remained unchanged. For 2005, however, she is operating on the Western Cyclades', now in the Hellenic Seaways colours. Internally she remains instantly recognisable as the *Stena Hibernia*, with facilities such as the themed Irish Bar and the

The **Stena Hibernia** (ex **St. Columba**) arrives at Holyhead in Stena Sealink livery. (*Miles Cowsill*)

The *Express Aphrodite* heads away from Sifnos in the new Hellenic Seaways colours in July 2005. *(Richard Seville)*

The *St. Julian* arrives at St.Helier during her brief season on the Channel Islands operations. *(Miles Cowsill)*

Pantry self-service still in place and much red Stena Line trim in evidence.

ST JULIEN 1989 - 1989
1977 - Usuki Shipyard, Usuki, Japan

The *St Julien* enjoyed only the briefest of UK careers when serving for the short-lived Weymouth Maritime Services in 1989. She had been constructed in Japan as AG Ems' *Emsland*, but had led a notably nomadic career, regularly being chartered out, including a short spell with Emeraude Line in 1984. In 1986 she was sold to Scandi Line for service across the Oslofjord from

The *Nura Nova* alongside at Alcudia in August 2003. *(Richard Seville)*

Sandefjord to Stromstad as the *Bohus*. It was from this operation that she was chartered to newly formed WMS for use from Weymouth to the Channel Islands. When WMS failed after their first season, she was sold to Bornholm Express to launch a competitive service to well-established Bornholmstrafikken between Ystad and Ronne. This too was unsuccessful, and in 1992 she was acquired by Tourship to inaugurate their new Elba Ferries subsidiary. As the *Elba Nova*, she ran on the highly competitive Piombino to Portaferraio route until replaced by the fast-craft *Elba Express* in 1995. Three years of lay-up followed before she was eventually sold to Iscomar. With a quick change of name *to Nura Nova*, she established their first passenger route from Alcudia to Mahon in the Balearics. She remains on the two-hour crossing today, where her interior largely retains its Tourship styling.

STENA NORMANDICA 1979 – 1985
St Brendan 1985 – 1990
1974 - Rickmers Werft, Bremerhaven, Germany

Commissioned by Stena Line as one of a quartet of high-capacity ferries built for the charter market, the *Stena Normandica* was delivered in late 1974. As intended, she served a wide variety of operators in her early career, visiting not only northern Europe but also the Mediterranean and north America. UK operators during this period included both Normandy Ferries and North Sea Ferries. In early 1979 Sealink chartered her for use between Fishguard and Rosslare, initially as a short-term measure until the

arrival of a new purpose-built vessel, the *St David*. However, the *Stena Normandica* proved so suitable for the link that she was retained and the *St David* was deployed elsewhere! Despite this, she never received the full Sealink UK blue-hulled livery, remaining in a unique white scheme. She was ultimately purchased in 1985 after the privatisation of Sealink and was renamed the *St Brendan*. Five years later, in late 1989, in advance of her displacement by the new *Felicity*, she was sold to Moby Lines of Italy with delivery in early 1990. As the *Moby Vincent* she has since been closely associated with the four-hour Livorno to Bastia route, but has seen periods out on charter – to Silja Line in 1993 and to Comanav in 1997. A sister, the *Reine Astrid* (q.v.) was also acquired by Moby in 1996 and renamed the *Moby Kiss*, but she never saw service with the Italian company, immediately

The wintry sunshine captures the **Stena Normandica** leaving Fishguard for Rosslare. *(Miles Cowsill)*

The *Moby Vincent* at speed en route to Bastia, September 2004. *(Richard Seville)*

RMT originally took the *Reine Astrid* on charter but such was her freight capacity that they later purchased her for service on the Ostend – Dover link. *(John Hendy)*

being chartered out. Like other members of the fleet, the *Moby Vincent* now wears a unique hull design, which in her case depicts a family of whales at the beach - complete with a parasol and beach balls! Although her internal layout is little altered, all her facilities have been refitted in the trademark Moby cool blue colour scheme.

STENA NAUTICA 1982 - 1983
Reine Astrid 1983 - 1997
1975 - Rickmers Werft Bremerhaven, Germany

The *Reine Astrid* was the final vessel of a quartet commissioned by Stena Line for the charter market, debuting as the *Stena Nordica*.

With double freight decks, each of the vessels was instantly in demand, and between 1975 and 1982 the *Stena Nordica* saw a wide variety of charters including several stints with both Marine Atlantic in Canada and Greece's Hellas Ferries (no relation to the current company). In 1982 she was renamed the *Stena Nautica* and chartered to RMT for service from Ostend to Dover, where her freight capacity proved invaluable. She was later purchased by the Belgians and gained the traditional name of *Reine Astrid* in March 1983. She served the company throughout their different partnerships and moved her UK base to Ramsgate in 1994 upon the alliance with Sally Line. She continued in service until withdrawn in October 1996 with damage to her bulbous bow after colliding with her berth at Ramsgate. With the demise of the company

The **Al Mansour** rounds the pier at Algeciras in May 2003. *(Richard Seville)*

imminent, she was not repaired but instead sold to Moby Lines. Although renamed the *Moby Kiss* she did not enter service for Moby, but was instead chartered to Comanav for use from Tangiers to Algeciras as the *Al Mansour*, being purchased the following year. Internally she remains remarkably unchanged from her Belgian days, retaining the interior installed by Studio Acht to bring her in line with the new *Prins Filip*. The only notable change is the conversion of her former cinema into a luxurious VIP Saloon, finished in traditional Moroccan style.

SVEA 1966 – 1968
Hispania 1968 – 1972
Saga 1972 – 1978
1966 - Ab Lindholmens, Gothenburg, Sweden

The *Svea* was delivered in 1966 as Svea Line's contribution to the England Sweden Line consortium and was deployed from Tilbury to Gothenburg. Although exceedingly elegant both internally and externally, together with her two sisters, the *Saga* and the *Patricia*, the stern-only loading *Svea* was unfortunately out-moded from the start. New upstart Tor Line aggressively eroded Svea Line's market and just two years after her delivery they withdrew and sold her to Swedish Lloyd. She became the *Hispania* and joined the *Patricia* on their Southampton to Bilbao route. The expected traffic never materialised however, and she moved back to the North Sea in 1970, taking her sister's name, *Saga*, in 1972. The original *Saga* had previously been sold to Stena Line. In 1978 Swedish Lloyd too succumbed to Tor Line's modern operations, and the *Saga* was sold to Minoan Lines, to join her one-time rival, the *Tor Anglia* (q.v.) in the expanding fleet. Minoan went on to acquire the original *Saga* too, re-uniting the two sisters. As the *Knossos*, the former *Svea* served in both the Aegean and the Adriatic for Minoan for twenty years. In 1998, together with her sister, she was sold to Korfez Shipping of Turkey, who renamed them *Captain Zaman I* and 'II' and deployed them from Brindisi to Igoumenitsa. Subsequently moved to the Black Sea, the *Captain Zaman II* was chartered to Comanav in both 2001 and 2002, before sale to Croatia's newly formed Blue Line in 2003.

The distinctive and attractive looking *Svea* is seen here at Gothenburg. (*Bruce Peter collection*)

The *Ancona* at speed off her namesake port, July 2004. (*Richard Seville*)

Renamed the *Ancona* she offers an unmissable travel experience sailing overnight between Split and her namesake port, still boasting beautiful wooden-panelled interiors complete with many original fittings.

TOR BRITANNIA 1975 – 1990
Prince of Scandinavia 1990 - 2003
1975 – Flender Werft, Lubeck, Germany

Delivered in 1975 to Tor Line, the hugely popular *Tor Britannia* was a mainstay of North Sea ferry services for no less than 28 years. Initially serving the triangular Immingham (later Felixtowe) –

Gothenburg – Amsterdam route, she came under DFDS control in 1981 following a failed merger between Tor Line and Sweden's Sessan Linjen. Although much of the artwork that had originally filled her interior was removed at this stage, she remained elegantly outfitted. However, in late 1990 she was dispatched to Hamburg for complete internal rebuilding, emerging as the *Prince of Scandinavia*. Her first taste of Mediterranean service came in 1996, when chartered to Cotunav to run between Italy and Tunisia. After spending her last three years on the Newcastle to Ijmuiden crossing, she was sold in late 2003 to Moby Lines, as a replacement for the damaged *Moby Magic*. Re-christened the *Moby Drea*, after owner Vincenzo Onorato's son, Andrea, she has become the

The *Tor Hollandia* makes a distinctive sight as she arrives off the Suffolk coast from Sweden. *(FotoFlite)*

The *Moby Drea* berthing at the Italian port of Livorno, September 2004. *(Richard Seville)*

flagship of the fleet. Moby Lines have made colourful hull designs their trademark, and the *Moby Drea* is painted in their most adventurous scheme yet. Her hull features the Looney Tunes characters – Wile Coyote, Tweetie-Pie, Taz, Bugs Bunny and Daffy Duck - whilst Silvester the Cat adorns her funnel! Although not to the taste of some, there is no doubt Moby's eye-catching schemes capture the public's imagination, generating valuable publicity for the company. Internally, her accommodation has been thoroughly refreshed, with changes including new cabins added in the former shop and games arcade, a new pizza bar installed in the former conference rooms and a dedicated Children's World created in the Jolly Roger Cafe

TOR HOLLANDIA 1967 - 1975
1967 – Flender Werft, Lubeck, Germany

When she debuted on the North Sea in 1967, the *Tor Hollandia* truly revolutionised the ferry market. Ordered for Tor Line, the new joint venture between Trans Oil and Rex Shipping, together with her earlier sister, the *Tor Anglia*, she brought drive- through design to the North Sea for the first time. Tor Line quickly captured traffic from the established operators Ellerman Wilson, Rederi AB Svea and Swedish Lloyd, and indeed were so successful at doing so that their rivals were driven out of business by 1973, 1971 and 1977 respectively. By the time of the latter, the original Tor Line twins had been replaced by the *Tor Britannia* (q.v.) and *Tor Scandinavia* of 1975/6, and the *Tor Hollandia* had been sold to Minoan Lines. She became the Cretan company's first modern car ferry in 1975, and was to remain in their fleet until 1999. She initially served Minoan's core Piraeus to Heraklion route in unaltered format, but was heavily rebuilt in 1989/90 to prepare her for a new, long-distance route from Italy to the Turkish port of Kusadasi. During this reconstruction, she was extended aft to include tiered sundecks and a new pool, while her original wooden panelled interiors were removed and she was fitted out with chrome, mirrors and pastel tones. Only her tiny observation lounge retained its original decor. She ended her Minoan service on a new domestic route to the Cyclades before sale in 1999 to Fragline. A long established Greek family concern, Fragline deployed her on their route from Brindisi to

The **Ouranos** berthed at Costa Morena, Brindisi, during July 2003. *(Richard Seville)*

Igoumenitsa under the name *Ouranos*. With Fragline under heavy pressure from competitors with more modern tonnage, her season has been reduced to just a few summer months, and for the remainder of the year she can usually be found laid up at Keratsini, close to Piraeus' Great Harbour.

ULSTER QUEEN 1967 - 1982
1967 - Cammel Laird Ltd, Birkenhead, UK

The *Ulster Queen* was a victim of outmoded design even before she was delivered. The stern-only loading vessel, with limited freight capacity and two-class accommodation, was commissioned by the Belfast Steamship Co, together with her twin, the *Ulster Prince*, for the overnight Belfast to Liverpool connection. In 1971, the

An early publicity photograph of the **Tor Hollandia**. *(Bruce Peter collection)*

company was taken over by P&O and in 1978 she was repainted in their light blue colours. However, the route was losing money and in 1981 the axe fell. Laid up in Ostend, the twins were offered for sale, and the *Ulster Queen* was quickly sold to Greek interests. As the *Med Sea*, she only saw limited service before being laid up again at Elefsis. During 1986/87, she served in the Red Sea as the *Al Kahera* and then the *Ala-Eddin* before being acquired by Hellenic Mediterranean in 1988. She spent a decade linking Greece and Italy as their *Poseidonia* before being laid up in 1998 in Elefsis Bay. As HML struggled to obtain more modern tonnage, she was re-activated in 2002 to again link Patras and Brindisi, presenting a stark contrast to the modern rival tonnage and remaining surprisingly unaltered internally from her Irish Sea days For 2004 she was due

to operate as HML's only vessel, but having been moved to Patras to commence services, she suffered serious mechanical problems and had to return to Piraeus, leaving HML without any ships. She laid-up until early 2005, when she left Piraeus for an unkown destination.

VIKING I 1964 – 1976
Viking Victory 1976 – 1983
1964 - Kaldnes Mek. Verksted A/S, Tönsberg, Norway

When the *Viking I* launched Otto Thoresen's routes from Southampton to Cherbourg and Le Havre, bringing drive-through services to the Western Channel, she and her two sisters were hugely

The *Ulster Queen* and sister ship *Ulster Prince* (seen here in 1980) operated the overnight service between Liverpool and Belfast. *(John Hendy)*

The *Poseidonia* lashed to a line of redundant cruise ships in Elefsis Bay, February 2003. *(Richard Seville)*

successful. She has, however, outlived the connections, which were closed by P&O Ferries in December 2004. That all three of the original Vikings survive today is testament to the success of their Knud.E.Hanson design. The *Viking I* became the *Viking Victory* in 1976 when she inaugurated services from Portsmouth, and she remained in the fleet until 1983 when sold to Cypriot interests to become the *Sun Boat*. She subsequently carried the names *Caravan*, *Vasmed* and *Sunny Boat* when used on a variety of Red Sea and Eastern Mediterranean routes, before making her debut on Adriatic service as the *European Glory* in 1990. The following year she began a long association with Hellenic Mediterranean Lines when

The **Viking II** leaves Southampton port for Cherbourg during her first season. *(Miles Cowsill collection)*

chartered as the *Neptunia* for use between Patras and Brindisi. She was bought in 1992, and as the *Media II* was a mainstay of their fleet for over a decade. In 2002 she passed to newcomer Palmier Ferries and was used initially from Brindisi to Igoumenitsa before transfer to the notorious Brindisi to Vlore connection. Having dominated the route at first, she now plays second fiddle to Agoudimos Lines' *Kapetan Alexandros A* (q.v), her former Townsend Thoresen fleet mate, *Doric Ferry*. Internally cabins have been added to the former Le Commandant Restaurant and the side lounges, but otherwise she is relatively little changed, complete with an abundance of wooden-panelled bulkheads.

The **Media V** raising her anchors as she moves to berth at Vlore, July 2003. *(Richard Seville)*

The *Earl William* (ex *Viking II*) is seen here in the bright sunshine at St. Peter Port in 1986. *(Miles Cowsill)*

VIKING II 1964 – 1976
Earl William 1976 - 1992
1964 - Kaldnes Mek. Verksted A/S, Tönsberg, Norway

The second of Thoresen's revolutionary 'Vikings', the *Viking II* spent the first thirteen years of her career sailing between Southampton, Cherbourg and Le Havre, but is more recently remembered as Sealink's *Earl William*. Acquired in late 1976 for use on the Channel Island services from Portsmouth, she was twice extended aft and in 1985 was luxuriously refitted for the ill-fated Starliner service. The new venture failed spectacularly, and a disastrous joint-service with new rivals Channel Island Ferries ended in strikes, legal action and Sealink being banned from operating to the islands. Her last regular British route was the short-lived Liverpool to Dun Laoghaire crossing between 1988 and early 1990, but she remained in the fleet as a relief vessel until January 1992. With a flick of the paintbrush, she sailed to the Mediterranean as the *Pearl William* for use by European Seaways between Brindisi and Igoumenitsa, her route later being extended to the Turkish port of Cesme. In 1996 she became *the Mar Julia* and in 1997 she began sailing as the *Cesme Stern* on services to the Turkish port, but in July was arrested at Bari. She remained laid-up there, steadily deteriorating, until 2001, having been renamed as the *Windward II* in 2000. Seemingly against all odds, the name change indicated she had been sold for further service and the following year she was towed to a shipyard in Trogir, Croatia. Despite the work being interrupted due to financial issues, she sailed for the Caribbean in late 2003, only to be again arrested in Trinidad following a collision with a navy vessel. She is believed to remain laid-up today.

The *Windward II* laid up at Trogir, amidst financial wrangles, July 2003. *(Richard Seville)*

VIKING VISCOUNT 1976 – 1987
Pride of Winchester 1989 – 1994
1976 -Aalborg Værft A/S, Aalborg, Danmark

The third of the 'Super Viking' quartet delivered to Townsend Thoresen in 1975/6, the *Viking Viscount* spent her first decade running from Felixtowe to Zeebrugge with her sister, the *Viking Voyager* (q.v.). In 1985, the pair were switched to the Portsmouth to Cherbourg route, where they remained through the P&O takeover in 1987. 1989 saw the *Viking Viscount* renamed the *Pride of Winchester* in line with P&O European Ferries' new naming policy, but she continued at Portsmouth until 1994 when indirectly displaced by the Olau Line sisters *Olau Hollandia* and *Olau Britannia*. She was sold to newly formed LANE Lines of Greece, to inaugurate a link from Piraeus to the Western-Cretan port of Agios Nikolaos, via the island of Milos. Success ensued and although LANE has since been acquired by ANEK Lines, the *Vitzentzos Kornaros'* operations continue unchanged. Interestingly she retained her P&O blue hull for her first season, and even today retains the blue arrow along her superstructure, which has actually been incorporated into LANE's standard fleet livery. Although little changed structurally, internally she has been converted for two-class operation, with the open-plan forward lounge bar divided in two to provide dual facilities. Her cabin accommodation has also been increased with additional facilities re-installed into the one-time Club Class Lounge, which ironically had been created through removing cabins.

The **Viking Viscount** was originally built for the Felixstowe-Zeebrugge service. *(Miles Cowsill collection)*

The former Townsend Thoresen ship the **Viking Viscount** still retains very modern lines despite being some 30 years old. *(Miles Cowsill)*

The **Viking Voyager** approaches Felixstowe harbour during her early career with the company. *(Miles Cowsill collection)*

Just a few days after entering service, Saos Ferries' new **Samothraki** is pictured at Piraeus in July 2005. *(Richard Seville)*

VIKING VOYAGER 1976 – 1989
Pride of Cherbourg 1989 - 1994
1976 -Aalborg Værft A/S, Aalborg, Danmark

The *Viking Voyager's* early history is identical to that of her sister, the *Viking Viscount* (q.v.). She became the *Pride of Cherbourg* in 1989, and immediately prior to replacement served briefly as the *Pride of Cherbourg II*. After withdrawal in September 1994, she was sold quickly to Lineas Fred. Olsen, for use in their expanding Canary Islands network. Renamed the *Banaderos*, she launched a new route from Santa Cruz de Tenerife to Agaete on Gran Canaria. Internally, all her facilities were renamed on local themes, but the only significant change was the conversion of the aft restaurant to become an additional bar lounge. Lineas Fred. Olsen have since embraced fast craft technology, and in 2000 she was displaced from this route by two InCats. Renamed the *Barlovento*, she was moved to inaugurate another new connection, this time from Los Cristianos to Valverde on the island of El Hierro, whilst also providing additional sailings to La Gomera. She became the last conventional vessel in the fleet in 2003, and it was little surprise that she too was put up for sale. In October 2004 she was sold to Saos Ferries of Greece to replace the *Nisos Limnos*, originally the *Vortigern* (q.v.), for which she has been renamed the *Samothraki*. Sadly during her final years with Fred Olsen, she was not maintained to their usual standards, and internally was rather neglected. Although the main deck facilities were acceptable, the former Club Class lounge suffered from serious water leakage, and the upper recliner lounges were in extremely poor condition and closed off to passengers.

The *Vortigern* slips quietly into Folkestone from Boulogne. *(Miles Cowsill)*

The *Express Milos* heads out of Piraeus, October 2002. *(Richard Seville)*

VORTIGERN 1969 – 1987
1969 – Swan Hunter, Newcastle-upon-Tyne, UK

The *Vortigern* was British Rail's first multi-purpose train, car and passenger ferry, and was originally intended to be the lead-ship of no less than 25 multi-purpose vessels. Built for the winter Dover to Dunkirk rail service, she also offered peak season operation on the Dover to Boulogne car ferry route. With the opening of the new French terminal at Dunkirk West, only two train ferries were required to maintain services and from then on principally operated as a vehicle ferry except for relief duty. She became increasingly associated with the Folkestone station from the early 1980s, remaining there until declared surplus in 1987. After various relief services, she was sold in early 1988 to Lindos Lines of Greece who rebuilt her at the stern and added additional cabins. As the *Milos Express* she became the mainstay of their operations to her namesake island for over a decade. In 1999, Lindos Lines were swept up in the expansion of Minoan Flying Dolphins, and the *Milos Express* and her route were incorporated into Hellas Ferries' network, with a slight name change to *Express Milos*. However Hellas Ferries' ageing fleet began to shrink rapidly in the early 2000's. With withdrawal due to the infamous 35-year age limit for Greek domestic vessels looming, she was sold in early 2003 to Saos Ferries. Renamed the *Nisos Limnos*, she worked her last days on an elongated route from Laviron to Chios. Increasingly rundown, but surprisingly little altered in many areas from her UK days, this much-loved and remarkably reliable vessel was sold for breaking in Alang in January 2005.

ZEELAND 1984 - 1986
1973 - Ateliers & Chantiers du Havre, Le Havre, France

The *Marko Polo* appeared in British waters from 1984 on charter to SMZ for operation on the Harwich to Hook of Holland route. She had been constructed as the *Peter Wessel* in 1973 for Larvik Line's service from Larvik to Frederikshavn. SMZ required stop-gap tonnage prior to the arrival of the 1986 new-build *Koningin Beatrix*, to replace the 1968-built *Prinses Juliana* which had been sold earlier. The ship was renamed *Zeeland* for the duration of her charter, and operated with a non-standard all-white livery but with SMZ funnel colours. During her time at the Hook, she operated as a two-class vessel. Upon completion of this charter, she was sold to Stena Line for use as the *Stena Nordica* on their triangular Gothenburg – Frederikshavn – Moss route. She was quickly replaced by larger tonnage, and passed to Jadrolinija in 1988 becoming their *Marko Polo*. The Balkan wars severely disrupted Jadrolinija's operations and in order to earn valuable capital whilst also keeping her out of danger, she was chartered out to TT-Line off-shoot TR Line for the 1992 season, retaining her Croatian name whilst linking Trelleborg and Rostock. She operated for Olympic Ferries in 1993 and Comanav in 1994 before returning to Jadrolinija service in 1995. Her interior is little changed from new, retaining a classic 1970s atmosphere, but Jadrolinija's excellent reputation for maintenance is reflected in her immaculate condition. Like the *Dubrovnik* (q.v.), she sees year-round service on Jadrolinija's trans-Adriatic and coastal express network.

The **Zeeland** seen at the Hook of Holland during her period of operation with SMZ. *(Miles Cowsill)*

The **Marko Polo** approaches Korcula in June 2004. *(Richard Seville)*

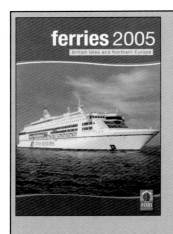